# 30 Gifts in 30 Days™

Mini Rounds Dishcloth, *page 9*

GW00458920

Tweedy Cables Throw, *page 28*

Chains of Love Cowl, *page 48*

## Table of Contents

Root Beer Post Scarf for Him, *page 44*

# Newborn Soft Puff Blanket

## Skill Level

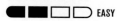 EASY

## Finished Measurements

26 inches wide x 30 inches long

## Materials

- Bernat Baby Blanket Tiny medium (worsted) weight acrylic yarn (3½ oz/316 yds/100g per ball):
    - 3 balls #14008 seedling
    - 2 balls #14013 spring lamb
- Size L/11/8mm crochet hook or size needed to obtain gauge
- Tapestry needle
- Measuring tape
- Scissors

## Gauge

10 sts = 4 inches; 7 rows = 4 inches

## Pattern Notes

Weave in loose ends as work progresses.

Blanket is crocheted from side to side holding 2 strands of yarn together throughout.

Edging is crocheted with 1 strand of yarn.

Chain-2 at beginning of row counts as first half double crochet unless otherwise stated.

## Special Stitch

**Puff stitch (puff st):** [Yo, insert hook in indicated ch or ch sp, yo, draw through ch or ch sp] twice, Yo, draw through all 5 lps on hook.

## Blanket

**Row 1 (RS): Holding 1 strand spring lamb and 1 strand seedling tog** (see Pattern Notes), ch 75, **puff st** (see Special Stitch) in **back bar** (see illustration) of 3rd ch from hook (2 sk chs count as hdc), [ch 1, sk next ch, puff st in next ch] 35 times, ch 1, sk next ch, hdc in last ch, turn. (36 puff sts, 2 hdc)

**Back Bar of Chain**

**Row 2: Ch 2** (see Pattern Notes), puff st in ch-1 sp, [ch 1, sk next puff st, puff st in next ch-1 sp] across to last 2 sts, ch 1, sk next puff st, hdc in last st, turn.

**Row 3:** Rep row 2.

**Row 4:** Ch 2, puff st in ch-1 sp, [ch 1, sk next puff st, puff st in next ch-1 sp] across to last 2 sts, ch 1, sk next puff st, hdc in last st, **changing color** *(see Stitch Guide)* to 2 strands seedling, turn. Fasten off spring lamb.

**Row 5:** Rep row 2.

**Row 6:** Ch 2, puff st in ch-1 sp, [ch 1, sk next puff st, puff st in next ch-1 sp] across to last 2 sts, ch 1, sk next puff st, hdc in last st, changing to 2 strands spring lamb, turn. Fasten off seedling strands.

**Row 7:** Rep row 2.

**Row 8:** Ch 2, puff st in ch-1 sp, [ch 1, sk next puff st, puff st in next ch-1 sp] across to last 2 sts, ch 1, sk next puff st, hdc in last st, changing to 2 strands seedling, turn. Fasten off spring lamb strands.

**Row 9:** Rep row 2.

**Row 10:** Ch 2, puff st in ch-1 sp, [ch 1, sk next puff st, puff st in next ch-1 sp] across to last 2 sts, ch 1, sk next puff st, hdc in last st, changing to 1 strand spring lamb and 1 strand seedling, turn. Fasten off seedling strand not in use.

**Rows 11–13:** [Rep row 2] 3 times.

**Rows 14–43:** [Rep rows 4–13] 3 times.

**Row 44:** Ch 2, puff st in next ch-1 sp, [ch 1, sk next puff st, puff st in next ch-1 sp] across to last 2 sts, ch 1, sk next puff st, hdc in last st, changing to **1 strand seedling** *(see Pattern Notes)*, turn. Fasten off spring lamb strand.

### Edging
With RS facing, ch 1, sk first st, 2 sc in next ch-1 sp, *[ch 1, sk puff st, sc in next ch-1 sp] across to last 2 sts, ch 1, sk last puff st, (sc, ch 1, sc) around post of hdc st, turn to work across ends of rows, [ch 1, sc around post of next hdc st] across to last row*, ch 1, (sc, ch 1, sc) around post of last hdc st, turn to work across foundation ch, sc in ch-1 sp before first puff st, rep from * to * once, ch 1, sc around post of last hdc st, ch 1, join with sl st in beg sc. Fasten off. *(164 sc, 160 ch-1 sps)* ●

# Snowcapped Baby Hat

## Skill Level
 EASY

## Finished Measurements
13 inches in circumference x 5 inches tall (with brim folded up)

## Gauge
15 sts = 4 inches; 12 rows = 4 inches

## Materials

**4**
**MEDIUM**

- Bernat Baby Blanket Tiny medium (worsted) weight acrylic yarn (3½ oz/316 yds/100g per ball):
  - 1 ball #14003 polar bear
- Size H/8/5mm crochet hook or size needed to obtain gauge
- Tapestry needle
- Stitch marker
- Measuring tape
- Scissors

## Pattern Notes

Weave in loose ends as work progresses.

Mark first stitch of round; move marker up with each round.

Work in continuous rounds; do not turn or join unless otherwise stated.

Join with slip stitch as indicated unless otherwise stated.

## Cap

**Rnd 1 (RS):** Ch 1, 8 sc in **back bar of ch** (see illustration), do not join, **place marker in first sc made** (see Pattern Notes), **do not join** (see Pattern Notes). (8 sts)

**Back Bar of Chain**

**Rnd 2:** [2 sc in **front lp** (see Stitch Guide) of next st, 2 sc in **back lp** (see Stitch Guide) of next st] 4 times. *(16 sts)*

**Rnd 3:** [2 sc in front lp of next st, sc in front lp of next st, 2 sc in back lp of next st, sc in back lp of next st] 4 times. *(24 sts)*

**Rnd 4:** [2 sc in front lp of next st, sc in front lp of each of next 2 sts, 2 sc in back lp of next st, sc in back lp of each of next 2 sts] 4 times. *(32 sts)*

**Rnd 5:** [2 sc in front lp of next st, sc in front lp of each of next 3 sts, 2 sc in back lp of next st, sc in back lp of each of next 3 sts] 4 times. *(40 sts)*

**Rnd 6:** [2 sc in front lp of next st, sc in front lp of each of next 4 sts, 2 sc in back lp of next st, sc in back lp of each of next 4 sts] 4 times. *(48 sts)*

**Rnd 7:** [Sc in front lp of each of next 6 sts, sc in back lp of each of next 6 sts] 4 times.

**Rnds 8–16:** Rep rnd 7.

**Rnd 17:** Sc in back lp of each st around.

**Rnd 18:** Rep rnd 17.

**Rnd 19:** Sc in back lp of each st around, **join** (see Pattern Notes) in back lp of beg st. Fasten off.

## Finishing

Turn rnds 17–19 up to form brim. ●

# One Step Baby Booties

## Skill Level

 ■■□□ EASY

## Finished Measurement

3½ inches long

## Materials

- King Cole Cherished DK light (light worsted) weight acrylic yarn (3½ oz/273 yds/100g per skein):
    1 skein #1410 white
- Size E/4/3.5mm crochet hook or size needed to obtain gauge
- Tapestry needle
- Stitch marker
- ¼-inch-wide white double-face satin ribbon: 48 inches
- Measuring tape
- Scissors

## Gauge

10 sts = 2 inches; 10 rows = 2 inches

## Pattern Note

Weave in loose ends as work progresses.

## Special Stitches

**Single crochet decrease-1 (sc dec-1):** [Insert hook in back lp of next st, yo, draw through] twice, yo, draw through all 3 lps on hook. *(1 st dec)*

**Single crochet decrease-2 (sc dec-2):** [Insert hook in back lp of next st, yo, draw through] 3 times, yo, draw through all 4 lps on hook. *(2 sts dec)*

## Bootie

**Make 2.**

**Row 1 (WS):** Leaving 15-inch strand at beg for sewing, ch 33, sc in **back lp** *(see Stitch Guide)* of 2nd ch from hook and in back lp of each of next 5 chs, ch 2, sk next 2 chs, sc in back lp of each of next 7 chs, 2 sc in back lp of each of next 2 chs *(shapes heel)*, sc in back lp of each of next 7 chs, ch 2, sk next 2 chs, sc in back lp of each of last 6 chs, turn. *(30 sts, 2 ch-2 sps)*

**Row 2 (RS):** Ch 1, sc in back lp of each of first 6 sts, ch 2, sk next ch-2 sp, sc in back lp of each of next 8 sts, 2 sc in back lp of each of next 2 sts, sc in back lp of each of next 8 sts, ch 2, sk next ch-2 sp, sc in back lp of each of last 6 sts, turn. *(32 sts, 2 ch-2 sps)*

**Row 3:** Ch 1, sc in back of each of first 6 sts, ch 2, sk next ch-2 sp, sc in back lp of each of next 20 sts, ch 2, sk next ch-2 sp, sc in back lp of each of last 6 sts, turn.

**Rows 4–10:** [Rep row 3] 7 times.

**Row 11:** Sl st in back lp of each of first 6 sts, sl st in back lp of each of next 2 chs, sc in back lp of each of next 20 sts, leaving last 2 chs and last 5 sts unworked, turn. *(20 sc)*

**Row 12:** Ch 1, sc in back lp of each of first 20 sts, leaving sl sts unworked, turn.

**Row 13:** Ch 1, sc in back lp of each st across, turn.

**Rows 14–16:** [Rep row 13] 3 times.

**Row 17:** Ch 1, sc in back lp of each of first 4 sts, **sc dec-1** *(see Special Stitches) (shapes side of toe)*, sc in back lp of each of next 8 sts, sc dec-1 *(shapes side of toe)*, sc in back lp of each of last 4 sts, turn. *(18 sts)*

**Row 18:** Ch 1, sc in back lp of each of first 3 sts, **sc dec-2** *(see Special Stitches)*, sc in back lp of each of next 3 sts *(place marker in sp before next st)*, sc in back lp of each of next 3 sts, sc dec-2, sc in back lp of each of last 3 sts. Fasten off, leaving long end for sewing. *(14 sts)*

## Finishing

Fold foundation ch row in half, RS facing, then with beg strand, sew row tog to form back of Bootie.

With ending strand, sew seam across ends of rows from row 18 to row 11. Push seam at row 18 down so that it touches marker; then sew toe opening closed sewing across row 18.

Turn Bootie RS out.

Cut 1 strand of ribbon 24 inches long; weave ribbon through ch-2 sps. Tie ends in bow; trim ends as desired.

Fold down cuff. ●

# Dainty Lace Magnet Buttons

## Skill Level
■■□□ **EASY**

## Finished Measurement
1½ inches in diameter

## Materials
- Aunt Lydia's Classic Crochet size 10 crochet cotton (400 yds per ball):
    1 ball #001 white
- Size 7/1.65mm steel crochet hook or size needed to obtain gauge
- 4 (1½-inch) extra-strength magnets
- Tapestry needle
- Clear-drying craft glue
- Measuring tape
- Scissors

**0 LACE**

Scribble Lace

Feathered Lace

Blossom Lace

Picot Lace

## Gauge

31 sts = 4 inches; rnds 1 and 2 = ¾ inch

## Pattern Notes

Weave in loose ends as work progresses.

Join with slip stitch as indicated unless otherwise stated.

Chain-4 at beginning of round counts as first double crochet and chain-1 unless otherwise stated.

Chain-3 at beginning of round counts as first double crochet unless otherwise stated.

## Special Stitch

**Picot:** Ch 3, insert hook through front lp of last sl st from top to bottom then through same st as last sl st, yo, pull through sts and lp on hook.

## Feathered Lace

**Rnd 1 (RS):** Ch 3, join in beg ch to form ring, **ch 4** (see Pattern Notes), [dc in ring, ch 1] 7 times, **join** (see Pattern Notes) in 3rd ch of beg ch-4. (8 dc, 8 ch-1 sps)

**Rnd 2:** Sl st in ch-1 sp as last sl st, ch 1, 3 sc in same ch-1 sp, [sk next dc, 3 sc in next ch-1 sp] 7 times, sk beg sl st, join in beg sc. (24 sc)

**Rnd 3:** [Ch 7, sl st in next sc] 23 times, ch 7, join in same st as beg ch-7. (24 ch-7 sps)

**Rnd 4:** Sl st in each of first 3 chs, sl st in ch-7 sp, **ch 3** (see Pattern Notes), dc in same ch-7 sp as last sl st, [dc in next ch-7 sp, 2 dc in next ch-7 sp] 11 times, dc in last ch-7 sp, join in top of beg ch-3. Fasten off. (36 dc)

## Picot Lace

**Rnds 1 & 2:** Rep rnds 1 and 2 of Feathered Lace.

**Rnd 3:** [Ch 7, sk next sc, sl st in next sc, **picot**—see Special Stitch] 11 times, ch 7, sk last sc, (sl st, picot) in same sc as beg ch-7. (12 ch-7 lps, 12 picots)

**Rnd 4:** Sl st in each of first 3 chs, sl st in ch-7 sp, **ch 3** (see Pattern Notes), 2 dc in same ch-7 sp as last sl st, [3 dc in next ch-7 sp] 11 times, join in top of beg ch-3. Fasten off. (36 dc)

## Scribble Lace

**Rnds 1 & 2:** Rep rnds 1 and 2 of Feathered Lace.

**Rnd 3:** [Ch 9, sk next 2 sc, sl st in next sc, **picot**—see Special Stitch, ch 9, sk next 2 sc, sl st in next sc] 4 times (last sl st will be in same st as beg ch-9). (8 ch-9 lps, 4 picots)

**Rnd 4:** Sl st in each of first 3 chs, sl st in ch-9 sp, ch 1, 2 sc in same sp as last sl st, *ch 3, sk picot, 2 sc in next ch-9 sp, ch 1, tr in sl st before next ch-9 lp, ch 1**, 2 sc in next ch-9 lp, rep from * around, ending last rep at **, join in beg sc. (4 tr, 16 sc, 8 ch-1 sps, 4 ch-3 sps)

**Rnd 5: Ch 3** (see Pattern Notes), *dc in next sc, 3 dc in next ch-3 sp, dc in each of next 2 sc, dc in next ch-1 sp, sk next tr, dc in next ch-1 sp**, dc in next sc, rep from * around, ending last rep at **, join in top of beg ch-3. Fasten off. (36 dc)

## Blossom Lace

**Rnds 1 & 2:** Rep rnds 1 and 2 of Feathered Lace.

**Rnd 3:** [Ch 4, sk next st, sl st in next st] 12 times (last sl st will be in same st as beg ch-4). (12 ch-4 sps)

**Rnd 4:** Sl st in first ch, sl st in next ch-4 sp, [ch 4, sl st in next ch-4 sp] 12 times (last sl st will be in same ch-4 sp as beg ch-4). (12 ch-4 sps)

**Rnd 5:** Sl st in ch-4 sp, **ch 3** (see Pattern Notes), 2 dc in same sp as last sl st, 3 dc in each rem ch-4 sp around, join in top of beg ch-3. Fasten off. (36 dc)

## Finishing

Gently stretching lace to fit, glue rnds 1 and 2 to center of magnet; then glue last rnd to sides of magnet. ●

# Flower Mound Coaster Set

## Skill Level

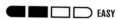 EASY

## Finished Measurement

4¼ inches in diameter

## Materials

- Bernat Handicrafter Cotton medium (worsted) weight cotton yarn (1¾ oz/80 yds/50g per ball): 1 ball each #1002 off-white, #1530 country red, #1699 tangerine and #1743 red
- Size H/8/5mm crochet hook or size needed to obtain gauge
- Tapestry needle
- Stitch marker
- Measuring tape
- Scissors

## Gauge

Rnds 1–4 = 4 inches

## Pattern Notes

Weave in loose ends as work progresses.

Join with slip stitch as indicated unless otherwise stated.

Chain-4 at beginning of round counts as first double crochet and chain-1 unless otherwise stated.

## Special Stitch

**Petal:** (Sc, ch 1, 2 dc, ch 1 sc) in indicated st.

## Coaster

**Make 1 each off-white and red, off-white and country red, and off-white and tangerine.**

**Rnd 1 (RS):** With off-white, ch 4, join in beg ch to form ring, **ch 4** *(see Pattern Notes)*, [dc in ring, ch 1] 7 times, **join** *(see Pattern Notes)* in 3rd ch of beg ch-4. Fasten off. *(8 dc, 8 ch-1 sps)*

**Rnd 2:** With RS facing, join 2nd color in any dc, ch 1, sc in same st as joining *(place marker in last st made)*, [ch 1, with hook in front of ch-1 sp, tr in beg ch-4 ring, ch 1, sc in next dc] 7 times, ch 1, with hook in front of ch-1 sp, tr in beg ch-4 ring, ch 1, join in beg sc. Fasten off. *(8 tr, 8 sc, 16 ch-1 sps)*

**Rnd 3:** With RS facing, with hook in front of a ch-1 sp after a sc, join off-white in off-white ch-1 sp 2 rnds below, ch 4, sk next tr, with hook in front of ch-1 sp, dc in same off-white ch-1 sp 2 rnds below as joining, [ch 1, sk next sc, with hook in front of ch-1 sp, dc in off-white ch-1 sp 2 rnds below, ch 1, sk next tr, with hook in front of ch-1 sp, dc in same off-white ch-1 sp 2 rnds below as last dc] 7 times, ch 1, join in 3rd ch of beg ch-4. Fasten off. *(16 dc, 16 ch-1 sps)*

**Rnd 4:** With RS facing, with hook in front of ch-1 sp, join 2nd color in marked 2nd color sc on rnd 2, ch 1, **petal** *(see Special Stitch)* in same sc as joining, [ch 1, sk (dc, ch-1, dc), with hook in front of next ch-1 sp, petal in next 2nd color sc 2 rnds below] 7 times, ch 1, sk last (dc, ch-1, dc), join in beg sc. Fasten off. *(8 petals, 8 ch-1 sps)*

**Rnd 5:** With RS facing, with hook in front of ch-1 sp between 2 petals, join off-white in off-white ch-1 sp 2 rnds below, ch 1, [sl st in **back lp** *(see Stitch Guide)* of each of next 6 sts on petal, with hook in front of ch-1 sp, sl st in off-white ch-1 sp 2 rnds below] 7 times, sl st in back lp of each of next 6 sts on last petal, join in beg ch-1 st. Fasten off. *(56 sl sts)* ●

# Mini Rounds Dishcloth

## Skill Level
■■□□ EASY

## Finished Measurement
5½ inches in diameter

## Materials
- Bernat Handicrafter Cotton medium (worsted) weight cotton yarn (solids: 1¾ oz/80 yds/ 50g; prints: 1½ oz/68 yds/ 43g per ball):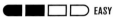
    1 ball each #1001 white and #2746 summer prints
- Bernat Handicrafter Cotton Stripes medium (worsted) weight cotton yarn (1½ oz/ 68 yds/43g per ball):
    1 ball # 4143 country stripes
- Size H/8/5mm crochet hook or size needed to obtain gauge
- Tapestry needle
- Measuring tape
- Scissors

## Gauge
Rnds 1–3 = 4 inches

## Pattern Notes
Weave in loose ends as work progresses.

Join with slip stitch as indicated unless otherwise stated.

Chain-3 at beginning of round counts as first double crochet unless otherwise stated.

Chain-4 at beginning of round counts as first double crochet and chain-1 unless otherwise stated.

Chain-5 at beginning of round counts as first double crochet and chain-2 unless otherwise stated.

## Special Stitches

**Beginning 3-double crochet group (beg 3-dc group): Ch 3** (see Pattern Notes), 2 dc in same ch sp as beg ch-3.

**3-double crochet group (3-dc group):** 3 dc in next ch sp.

## Dishcloth

**Make 1 each with first color white and 2nd color country stripes, with first color country stripes and 2nd color white, and with first color white and 2nd color summer print.**

**Rnd 1 (RS):** Starting with first color, ch 3, join in beg ch to form ring, **ch 4** (see Pattern Notes), [dc in ring, ch 1] 7 times, **join** (see Pattern Notes) in 3rd ch of beg ch-4. Fasten off. (8 dc, 8 ch-1 sps)

**Rnd 2:** With RS facing, join 2nd color in any ch-1 sp, **beg 3-dc group** (see Special Stitches), [sk next dc, **3-dc group** (see Special Stitches) in next ch-1 sp] 7 times, sk last dc, join in top of beg ch-3. Fasten off. (8 3-dc groups)

**Rnd 3:** With RS facing, join first color in sp between 2 3-dc groups, **ch 5** (see Pattern Notes), dc in same sp as joining, [ch 2, (dc, ch 2, dc) in sp between next 2 3-dc groups] 7 times, ch 2, join in 3rd ch of beg ch-5. Fasten off. (16 dc, 16 ch-2 sps)

**Rnd 4:** With RS facing, join 2nd color in any ch-2 sp, beg 3-dc group, [sk next dc, 3-dc group] 15 times, sk last dc, join in top of beg ch-3. Fasten off. (16 3-dc groups)

**Rnd 5:** With RS facing, join first color in sp between any 2 3-dc groups, ch 4, [sl st in sp between next 2 3-dc groups, ch 3] 15 times, join in first ch of beg ch-4. Fasten off. (64 sl sts) ●

# Dressy Dish Towel

**Skill Level**

� ■ ■ □ □ EASY

**Finished Measurement**
14½ inches long

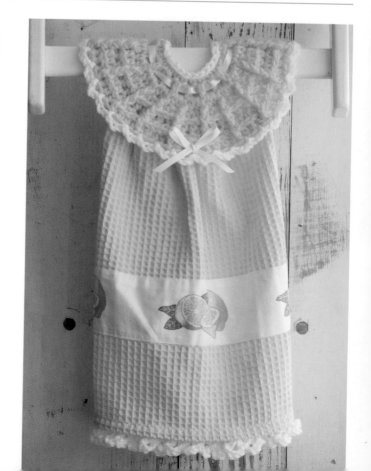

## Materials

- Premier Yarns Deborah Norville Everyday Soft medium (worsted) weight acrylic yarn (4 oz/203 yds/ 113g per skein):
    - 1 skein each #100-01 snow white and #100-27 lemon
- Size H/8/5mm crochet hook or size needed to obtain gauge
- Steel crochet hook small enough to go through manufacturer's seam stitch on dish towel (hook is not used for crocheting)
- Tapestry needle
- Sewing needle
- Matching sewing thread
- Stitch markers: 2
- Straight pins: 2
- ¾-inch shank white buttons: 2
- Matching lemon sewing thread
- ¼-inch-wide white double-face satin ribbon: 1⅔ yds
- 15-inch x 24-inch dish towel
- Measuring tape
- Scissors

## Gauge

13 sts = 4 inches; 9 rows = 4 inches

## Pattern Notes

Weave in loose ends as work progresses.

Join with slip stitch as indicated unless otherwise stated.

Chain-1 at beginning of round does not count as a stitch.

Half double crochet stitches have 3 horizontal strands across the top called front loop, back loop and bar. With RS facing, crocheting behind the front loop and back loop into the bar pushes the front loop and back loop to the front of the fabric.

## Special Stitch

**Bar half double crochet (bar hdc):** Yo, insert hook through **bar** *(see Pattern Notes)* of indicated st, yo, draw through, yo, draw through all 3 lps on hook.

## Dish Towel

### Yoke

**Rnd 1:** With lemon, leaving 10-inch strand at beg for sewing, ch 31, sc in **back bar** *(see illustration)* of 2nd ch from hook and in back bar of each rem ch across, being careful not to twist sts, **join** *(see Pattern Notes)* in beg st to form ring. *(30 sc)*

**Back Bar of Chain**

**Rnd 2: Ch 1** *(see Pattern Notes)*, hdc in same st as beg ch-1, [ch 2, sk next st, hdc in next st] twice, [ch 1, hdc in next st] 5 times, [ch 2, sk next st, hdc in next st] 5 times, [ch 1, hdc in next st] 5 times, [ch 2, sk next st, hdc in next st] twice, ch 2, sk last st, join in beg hdc. *(20 hdc, 20 ch sps)*

**Rnd 3:** Ch 1, hdc in same st as beg ch-1, *2 hdc in next ch sp, hdc in next st, rep from * around to last ch sp, 2 hdc in last ch sp, join in beg hdc. *(60 hdc)*

**Rnd 4:** Ch 1, **fpdc** *(see Stitch Guide)* around post of same st as beg ch-1, *hdc in each of next 2 sts, fpdc around post of next st, rep from * around to last 2 sts, hdc in each of last 2 sts, join in beg fpdc.

**Rnd 5:** Ch 1, *fpdc around post of post st, **bar hdc** *(see Special Stitch)* in each of next 2 sts, rep from * around, join in beg fpdc.

**Rnd 6:** Ch 1, fpdc around post of post st, [hdc in each of next 3 sts, fpdc around post of same post st as last hdc *(1 st inc)*] twice, place marker in last post st made to mark beg of front bodice, [hdc in each of next 3 sts, fpdc around post of same post st as last hdc *(1 st inc)*] 5 times, place marker in last post st made to mark end of front bodice, [hdc in each of next 3 sts, fpdc around post of same post st as last hdc *(1 st inc)*] 12 times, hdc in each of last 2 sts, hdc in same st as beg fpdc *(1 st inc)*, join in beg fpdc. *(80 sts)*

**Rnd 7:** Ch 1, *fpdc around post of post st, bar hdc in each of next 3 sts, rep from * around, join in beg fpdc. Fasten off.

With beg end, sew bottom of rnd 1 tog.

## Neck Edging
With Yoke right side up, join snow white in unused lp of foundation ch, sl st in each unused lp around, join in beg sl st. Fasten off. *(30 sl sts)*

## Yoke Edging
With Yoke upside down, join snow white in any hdc after a post st on rnd 7, ch 4, [sk next st, sl st in next st, ch 3] 39 times, join in first ch of beg ch-4. Fasten off. *(40 ch lps)*

## Dish Towel Skirt
Fold dish towel in half so top and bottom are touching; then cut across fold making 2 pieces 15 x 12 inches each.

With dish towel half to be used, fold cut end back ¼ inch twice. Using sewing needle and matching thread, sew seam across folds then sew ends of folds tog forming ring (where ends meet is center back of skirt).

Sew a button on each side of center back of skirt so that buttons are 3 inches apart.

With straight pins, mark front 10 inches of skirt waist, then sew marked section between Yoke front markers gathering excess dish towel in front to form full skirt look.

## Petticoat
***Note:** Petticoat is worked in manufacturer's bottom seam on dish towel.*

**Row 1 (RS):** Place dish towel right side up, WS facing, with steel hook, pull snow white lp through first st on manufacturer's seam, *drop lp from steel hook, place lp on larger hook, ch 2, sk next 2 seam sts, drop lp from larger hook, with steel hook pull, dropped lp through next seam st, rep from * across bottom of dish towel, adjusting sts if needed so last lp pulled through is in last seam st on dish towel, drop lp from steel hook, place lp on larger hook, turn.

**Row 2:** Ch 3, sl st in first ch-2 sp, *ch 3, sl st in next ch-2 sp, rep from * across, turn.

**Row 3:** Ch 3, sl st in first ch-3 sp, *ch 3, sl st in next ch-3 sp, rep from * across. Fasten off.

## Back Ribbon
Cut ribbon 48 inches long. Weave ribbon through ch sps on Yoke rnd 2, starting at yoke center back, adjust ribbon to make ends of equal length. Tie ends in bow; trim as desired.

## Front Bow
Cut ribbon 12 inches long. Referring to photo for placement, attach to front center of Yoke; adjust ribbon to make ends of equal length. Tie ends in bow; trim as desired. ●

# Twirling Trivet

## Skill Level

 EASY

## Finished Measurement

9 inches in diameter

## Materials

- Bernat Handicrafter Cotton medium (worsted) weight cotton yarn (1¾ oz/80 yds/50g per ball):
    1 ball #1699 tangerine
- Size H/8/5mm crochet hook or size needed to obtain gauge
- Tapestry needle
- Stitch marker
- Measuring tape
- Scissors

## Gauge

Motif = 3 inches in diameter

## Pattern Notes

Weave in loose ends as work progresses.

Join with slip stitch as indicated unless otherwise stated.

Work in continuous rounds; do not turn or join unless otherwise stated.

Chain-3 at beginning of round counts as first double crochet unless otherwise stated.

Current motif is the motif you are crocheting.

Joining motif is the motif you are joining to the current motif.

## Special Stitches

**Post cap:** Sl st in indicated post st, ch 1, (fpdc, ch 1, fpdc) around post of same post st as last sl st.

**Motif join:** With WS of **joining motif** *(see Pattern Notes)* facing, insert hook through sl st made over a dc then with RS of **current motif** *(see Pattern Notes)* facing, insert hook through next dc on current motif, yo, draw through sts and lp on hook.

## Trivet

### First (Center) Motif

**Rnd 1 (RS):** Ch 4, 11 dc in 4th ch from hook *(3 sk chs count as a dc)*, **join** *(see Pattern Notes)* in top of beg ch-4. *(12 dc)*

**Rnd 2: Ch 3** *(see Pattern Notes)*, **fptr** *(see Stitch Guide)* around post of same st as beg ch-3, [dc in next st, fptr around post of same st as last dc] 11 times, **do not join** *(see Pattern Notes)*. *(24 sts)*

**Rnd 3:** [Sl st in next dc, **post cap** *(see Special Stitches)*] around, join in beg sl st. Fasten off.

## 2nd Motif

**Rnds 1 & 2:** Rep rnds 1 and 2 of First Motif.

**Rnd 3: Motif join** (*see Special Stitches*) to First Motif, on current motif, post cap in next post st, motif join to next sl st-over-dc on First Motif, [on current motif, post cap, sl st in next dc] twice, *(place marker in last sl st made)*, [post cap, sl st in next dc] 8 times, post cap, join in beg sl st. Fasten off.

## 3rd–6th Motifs

**Rnds 1 & 2:** Rep rnds 1 and 2 of First Motif.

**Rnd 3:** Motif join to marked st on last motif, on current motif, post cap, motif join to next sl st-over-dc on last motif, on current motif, post cap, [motif join to next sl st-over-dc on First Motif, on current

motif, post cap] twice, on current motif, sl st in next dc, post cap, sl st in next dc *(place marker in last sl st made)*, [post cap, sl st in next dc] 6 times, post cap, join in beg sl st. Fasten off.

## 7th Motif

**Rnds 1 & 2:** Rep rnds 1 and 2 of First Motif.

**Rnd 3:** Motif join to marked st on last motif, on current motif, post cap, motif join to next sl st-over-dc on last motif, on current motif, post cap, [motif join to next sl st-over-dc on First Motif, on current motif, post cap] twice, [motif join to next sl st-over-dc on 2nd Motif, on current motif, post cap] twice, [on current motif, sl st in next dc, post cap] 6 times, join in beg sl st. Fasten off. ●

# Soft Ringlets Chemo Cap

## Skill Level
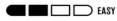 EASY

## Finished Measurements
20 inches in circumference x 8½ inches tall

## Materials

- Premier Yarns Deborah Norville Cotton Soft Silk medium (worsted) weight cotton/silk yarn (3 oz/154 yds/85g per skein):
    1 skein #950-10 turquoise
- Sizes G/6/4mm and K/10½/6.5mm crochet hooks or size needed to obtain gauge
- Tapestry needle
- Stitch marker
- 3½-inch cardboard square
- Measuring tape
- Scissors

## Gauge

**With larger hook:** 11 sts = 5 inches; 12 rows = 5 inches

## Pattern Notes

Weave in loose ends as work progresses.

Join with slip stitch as indicated unless otherwise stated.

Mark first stitch of round; move marker up with each round.

Work in continuous rounds; do not turn or join unless otherwise stated.

## Special Stitches

**Ringlet:** Yo 4 times, insert hook in indicated st, yo, draw through st, yo, draw through all 6 lps on hook.

**Ringlet decrease (ringlet dec):** Yo 4 times, [insert hook in sp between next 2 ringlets, yo, draw through] 2 times, yo, draw through all 7 lps on hook.

## Cap

**Rnd 1 (RS):** Leaving 10-inch strand at beg for sewing and with smaller hook, ch 74, sc in **back bar** (see illustration) of 2nd ch from hook and in back bar of each rem ch across, being careful not to twist sts, **join** (see Pattern Notes) in beg sc to form ring. (73 sc)

**Back Bar of Chain**

**Rnd 2:** Ch 1, sc in each st around, join in beg sc.

**Rnds 3 & 4:** [Rep rnd 2] 2 times.

**Rnd 5:** Ch 1, sc in each st around, join in **back lp** (see Stitch Guide) of beg sc.

**Rnd 6:** With larger hook, sk first sc, **ringlet** (see Special Stitches) in back lp of each of next 2 sts, [sk next sc, ringlet in back lp of next st, sk next sc, ringlet in back lp of each of next 2 sts] 14 times, **do not join, place marker** (see Pattern Notes). (44 ringlets)

**Rnd 7:** Ringlet in first ringlet, [ringlet in sp between next 2 ringlets] around.

**Rnd 8:** [Ringlet in sp between next 2 ringlets] around.

**Rnds 9–13:** [Rep rnd 8] 5 times.

**Rnd 14:** *[Ringlet in sp between next 2 ringlets] 9 times, **ringlet dec** (see Special Stitches), rep from * around. (40 ringlets)

**Rnd 15:** *[Ringlet in sp between next 2 ringlets] 8 times, ringlet dec, rep from * around. (36 ringlets)

**Rnd 16:** *[Ringlet in sp between next 2 ringlets] 7 times, ringlet dec, rep from * around. (32 ringlets)

**Rnd 17:** *[Ringlet in sp between next 2 ringlets] 6 times, ringlet dec, rep from * around. (28 ringlets)

**Rnd 18:** *[Ringlet in sp between next 2 ringlets] 5 times, ringlet dec, rep from * around. (24 ringlets)

**Rnd 19:** *[Ringlet in sp between next 2 ringlets] 2 times, ringlet dec, rep from * around. (18 ringlets)

**Rnd 20:** [Ringlet in sp between next 2 ringlets, ringlet dec] 6 times. (12 ringlets)

**Rnd 21:** [Ringlet dec] 6 times. Fasten off, leaving long strand for weaving. *(6 ringlets)*

Weave strand through rem 6 ringlets, pull tight to close and secure end.

With beg end, sew bottom of rnd 1 tog.

## Bow
**Row 1:** Leaving 15-inch strand at beg for sewing, ch 9, sc in back bar of 2nd ch from hook and in back bar of each rem ch across, turn. *(8 sc)*

**Row 2:** Ch 1, sc in each st across. Fasten off, leaving 10-inch strand for sewing.

With 10-inch strand, sew ends of rows tog to form ring.

Wrap yarn 20 times around cardboard. Fasten off.

Remove lps from cardboard, pull lps through ring so ring is at center of lps.

With beg 15-inch strand, sew front and back of ring tog along ring sides, catching lps in sts to help hold lps in place.

Sew Bow to Cap rnds 1–5 at rnd joinings. ●

---

# Blue Ridge Mountain Cap

## Skill Level
 EASY

## Finished Measurements
20 inches in circumference x 8 inches tall

## Materials
- King Cole Drifter DK light (DK) weight acrylic/cotton/wool yarn (3½ oz/328 yds/100g per skein): 1 skein #1368 Virginia
- Size G/6/4mm crochet hook or size needed to obtain gauge
- Tapestry needle
- Stitch marker
- Measuring tape
- Scissors

## Gauge
21 sts = 5 inches; 9 rows = 3 inches

## Pattern Notes
Weave in loose ends as work progresses.

Join with slip stitch as indicated unless otherwise stated.

Chain-1 at beginning of round does not count as a stitch.

Chain-2 at beginning of round does not count as a stitch.

## Cap
**Rnd 1 (RS):** Ch 1, 7 sc in **back bar of ch** *(see illustration)*, **join** *(see Pattern Notes)* in **front lp** *(see Stitch Guide)* of beg sc, *(place marker in front lp of beg sc where join was made)*. *(7 sc)*

**Back Bar of Chain**

**Rnd 2:** Sl st in front lp of each of next 6 sts, drop lp from hook, insert hook from back of fabric to front of fabric through **back lp** *(see Stitch Guide)* of next

Wyoming Drifter Cap,
*page 18*

st, place dropped lp on hook, draw lp to back of fabric, sl st in marked front lp.

**Rnd 3: Ch 1** *(see Pattern Notes)*, 2 dc in marked front lp, working behind sl sts of rnd 2 and into front lps of rnd 1 *(same front lps where sl sts on rnd 2 were made)*, 2 dc in each front lp around, join in top of beg dc. *(14 sts)*

**Rnd 4: Ch 2** *(see Pattern Notes)*, dc in same st as beg ch-2, **fptr** *(see Stitch Guide)* around post of same st as first dc, [dc in next st, fptr around post of same st] 13 times, join in front lp of first dc *(place marker in front lp of beg dc where join was made)*. *(28 sts)*

**Rnd 5:** Sl st in front lp of each of next 27 sts, drop lp from hook, insert hook from back of fabric to front of fabric through back lp of next st, place dropped lp on hook, draw lp to back of fabric, sl st in marked front lp.

**Rnd 6:** Ch 1, 2 dc in marked front lp, working behind sl sts of rnd 5 and into front lps of rnd 4 *(same front lps where sl sts on rnd 5 were made)*, 2 dc in each front lp around, join in top of beg dc. *(56 sts)*

**Rnd 7:** Ch 2, dc in same st as beg ch-2, [fptr around post of next st, dc in next st] around to last st, fptr around post of last st, join in front lp of beg dc *(place*

st marker in front lp of first dc where joining was made).

**Rnd 8:** Sl st in front lp of each of next 55 sts, drop lp from hook, insert hook from back of fabric to front of fabric through back lp of next st, place dropped lp on hook, draw lp to back of fabric, sl st in marked front lp.

**Rnd 9:** Ch 1, 2 dc in marked front lp, working behind sl sts of rnd 8 and into front lps of rnd 7 *(same front lps where sl sts on rnd 8 were made)*, [dc in next front lp of next st, 2 dc in next front lp of next st] 27 times, dc in front lp of last st, join in top of beg dc. *(84 sts)*

**Rnd 10:** Ch 2, dc in same st as beg ch-2, [fptr around post of next st, dc in next st] around to last st, fptr around of last st, join in front lp of first dc *(place st marker in front lp of first dc where join was made).*

**Rnd 11:** Sl st in front lp of each of next 83 sts, drop lp from hook, insert hook from back of fabric to front of fabric through back lp of next st, place dropped lp on hook, draw lp to back of fabric, sl st in marked front lp.

**Rnd 12:** Ch 1, dc in marked front lp, working behind sl sts of last rnd and into front lps of rnd 2 rnds below *(same front lps where sl sts on last rnd were made)*, dc in front lp of each st around, join in top of beg dc.

**Rnds 13–24:** [Rep rnds 10–12] 4 times.

**Rnd 25:** Ch 1, **reverse sc** *(see Stitch Guide)* in each st around, join in beg st. Fasten off. ●

# Wyoming Drifter Cap

## Skill Level

 EASY

## Finished Measurements

22 inches in circumference x 9 inches tall

## Materials

- King Cole Drifter DK light (DK) weight acrylic/cotton/wool yarn (3½ oz/328 yds/100g per skein): 1 skein #1370 Wyoming
- Sizes G/6/4mm and K/10½/6.5mm crochet hooks or size needed to obtain gauge
- Tapestry needle
- Stitch marker
- Measuring tape
- Scissors

## Gauge

**With larger hook:** 19 sts = 4 inches; 18 rows = 5 inches

## Pattern Notes

Weave in loose ends as work progresses.

Join with slip stitch as indicated unless otherwise stated.

Mark first stitch of round; move marker up with each round.

Work in continuous rounds; do not turn or join unless otherwise stated.

Chain-2 at beginning of round counts as first half double crochet unless otherwise stated.

## Special Stitch

**Slip stitch decrease (sl st dec):** [Insert hook in front lp of next st] twice, yo, draw through both sts and lp on hook.

## Cap

**Rnd 1 (RS):** Leaving 10-inch strand at beg for sewing and with smaller hook, ch 106, dc in **back bar** *(see illustration)* of 4th ch from hook *(3 sk chs count as a dc)* and in back bar of each rem ch across, being careful not to twist sts, **join** *(see Pattern Notes)* in top of beg dc to form ring. *(104 dc)*

**Back Bar of Chain**

**Rnd 2:** Ch 2 *(see Pattern Notes)*, [**fpdc** *(see Stitch Guide)* around post of next st, **bpdc** *(see Stitch Guide)* around post of next st] around to last st, fpdc around post of last st, join in top of beg ch-2.

**Rnds 3–7:** [Rep row 2] 5 times.

**Rnd 8:** With larger hook, sl st in **front lp** *(see Stitch Guide)* of st, **place marker in st just made** *(see Pattern Notes)*, sl st in front lp of each rem st around, **do not join, place marker** *(see Pattern Notes)*.

**Rnds 9–21:** [Rep rnd 8] 13 times.

**Rnd 22:** [Sl st in front lp of each of next 11 sts, **sl st dec** (*see Special Stitch*)] 8 times. (*96 sts*)

**Rnd 23:** Sl st in front lp of each st around.

**Rnd 24:** [Sl st in front lp of each of next 10 sts, sl st dec] 8 times. (*88 sts*)

**Rnd 25:** Rep rnd 23.

**Rnd 26:** [Sl st in front lp of each of next 9 sts, sl st dec] 8 times. (*80 sts*)

**Rnd 27:** Rep rnd 23.

**Rnd 28:** [Sl st in front lp of each of next 8 sts, sl st dec] 8 times. (*72 sts*)

**Rnd 29:** [Sl st in front lp of each of next 7 sts, sl st dec] 8 times. (*64 sts*)

**Rnd 30:** Rep rnd 23.

**Rnd 31:** [Sl st in front lp of each of next 6 sts, sl st dec] 8 times. (*56 sts*)

**Rnd 32:** [Sl st in front lp of each of next 5 sts, sl st dec] 8 times. (*48 sts*)

**Rnd 33:** Rep rnd 23.

**Rnd 34:** [Sl st in front lp of each of next 4 sts, sl st dec] 8 times. (*40 sts*)

**Rnd 35:** [Sl st in front lp of each of next 3 sts, sl st dec] 8 times. (*32 sts*)

**Rnd 36:** Rep rnd 23.

**Rnd 37:** [Sl st in each of next 2 sts, sl st dec in next 2 sts] 8 times. (*24 sts*)

**Rnd 38:** [Sl st in front lp of next st, sl st dec] 8 times. (*16 sts*)

**Rnd 39:** [Sl st dec] 8 times. Fasten off, leaving long strand for weaving. (*8 sts*)

## Finishing

Weave strand through rem 8 sts; pull tight to close and secure end.

With beg strand, sew bottom of rnd 1 tog. ●

# Twisted Pearl Choker

## Skill Level

 EASY

## Finished Measurement

12 inches long when twisted ropes are relaxed (choker stretches to 16 inches)

## Materials

- Aunt Lydia's Classic Crochet size 10 crochet cotton (400 yds per ball):
  - 1 ball #419 ecru
- Size 7/1.65mm steel crochet hook or size needed to obtain gauge
- Tapestry needle
- 12mm round white pearl bead
- 3mm gold spacer beads: 2
- Gold barrel clasp
- Waxed dental floss

## Gauge

In twisted pattern when rope is relaxed:
45 sts = 1 inch

## Pattern Note

Weave in loose ends as work progresses.

## Choker

### Beading Needle

To make beading needle, cut 8-inch piece of waxed dental floss. Hold ends of floss tog forming lp (*eye of needle*). Squeeze ends of floss tog so that they stick tog forming point of needle.

## Twisted Rope
**Make 2.**

With beading needle, string 1 end of barrel clasp onto yarn. Then leaving 12-inch end at beg for attaching beads, ch 84, push barrel clasp up to hook, 3 hdc in **back bar** (*see illustration*) of 2nd ch from hook (*barrel clasp is now attached to end of choker*), 3 hdc in back bar of each rem ch across to last 2 chs, (2 hdc, sc) in back bar of next ch, sl st in back bar of last ch. Fasten off. (*245 hdc, 1 sc*)

**Back Bar of Chain**

## Finishing

With beading needle and beg strand of 1 twisted rope, string first separator bead, pearl, 2nd separator bead. Then with beading needle and beg end of other twisted rope, string 2nd separator bead, pearl, first separator bead, creating 2 strings of thread running through beads in opposite directions. Adjust strands so that beads are touching first st of each twisted rope. Weave in ends of strands. Fasten off excess thread. ●

# Forget-Me-Not Alzheimer's Charm Bracelet

## Skill Level
 EASY

## Finished Measurement
9 inches long

## Materials
- Aunt Lydia's Classic Crochet size 10 crochet cotton (white: 400 yds per ball; solids: 350 yds per ball): 1 ball each #001 white, #421 goldenrod, #451 parakeet, #458 purple, #493 French rose and #495 wood violet
- Size 7/1.65mm steel crochet hook or size needed to obtain gauge
- Tapestry needle
- 1-inch cabone rings: 5
- 6/0 glass seed beads: 5 opaque yellow
- 6mm gold round jump rings: 1 pkg
- 6mm gold spring rings: 1 pkg
- 5 charms (see Pattern Notes)
- Jewelry pliers
- Waxed dental floss
- Materials for Crafted Charms
- 2-inch-long gold head pin
- 5 beads of choice with at least one bead's opening smaller than head on pin (beads should measure ¾–1 inch tall when strung (see Pattern Notes)

## Gauge
38 sts = 3 inches when crocheting around ring

Forget-me-not = ⅝ inch

## Pattern Notes
Charms can be made or purchased. Model was made using charms:
- Gold locket charm (for photo of loved one)
- Elephant charm (they never forget)
- Star charm (loved ones are a star to us)
- Crafted tassel charm (a symbol of respect)
- Crafted bead charm (loved ones are always beautiful)

Bead charm was crafted using:
- Gold heart bead (for love)
- Pearl bead (for value)
- Violet dice (for luck)
- 2 gold separator beads

Weave in loose ends as work progresses.

Join with slip stitch as indicated unless otherwise stated.

## Bracelet

### Beading Needle
To make beading needle, cut 8-inch piece of waxed dental floss. For eye of needle, fold ends of floss tog forming lp. Squeeze ends of floss tog so that they stick together forming point of needle.

### Forget-Me-Not
**Make 1 each in white, goldenrod, parakeet, French rose and wood violet.**

Leaving long end at beg, ch 3, being careful not to twist ch, **join** *(see Pattern Notes)* in beg ch to form ring, [ch 5, sl st in ring] 5 times. Fasten off, leaving long end for sewing. *(5 petals)*

Push long beg end through ring to RS of flower; with beading needle, string 1 bead on strand. Then with tapestry needle, sew bead to center of flower.

### Ring
**Make 5.**

Join purple in ring, ch 1, [10 sc around ring, drop lp from hook, push lp through jump ring, place lp back on hook, 10 sc around ring] twice, join in beg st. Fasten off. *(40 sts)*

### Finishing
With forget-me-not ending long strand, sew petals of 1 forget-me-not evenly sp inside each ring by inserting needle through back side of sc on ring.

With pliers and jump rings, connect forget-me-not rings tog so that 3 jump rings separate each forget-me-not ring. Attach spring ring to jump ring on 1 end of bracelet and attach 5 more jump rings to jump ring on other end of bracelet.

If charm does not have a spring ring, attach spring ring to charm, then attach charm to center jump ring between each forget-me-not ring. For last charm, sk 1 jump ring on end of bracelet where 6 jump rings are tog, attach last charm to next jump ring.

### Crafted Charms

#### Tassel
Cut 5 strands of wood violet and 5 strands of white each 3 inches long. Push strands through jump ring so that jump ring is in center of strands. Cut 1 strand of wood violet 6 inches long. Push ends of strands over jump ring forming Tassel with jump ring in middle. Tie 6-inch strand around top of Tassel just below jump ring. Trim Tassel as desired. Attach 1 jump ring to jump ring on Tassel; attach spring ring to last jump ring.

#### Bead Charm
Place bead with smallest opening on head pin; then place other beads of choice on pin. With pliers, bend tip of pin down inserting tip back through beads from last bead down to first bead, leaving enough pin above last bead to form lp. Shape pin to form lp; attach 1 jump ring to lp and 1 spring ring to jump ring. ●

# Glittering Gold Coin Purse

## Skill Level
 EASY

## Finished Measurements
4 inches wide x 3½ inches tall not counting clasp

## Materials
- Premier Yarns Wool-Free Lace super fine (fingering) weight acrylic/polyamide/glitter yarn (3½ oz/448 yds/100g per ball): 1 ball #95-205 gypsy bling
- Size D/3/3.25mm crochet hook or size needed to obtain gauge
- Tapestry needle
- Sewing needle
- Stitch marker
- Transparent nylon sewing thread
- 3⅕-inch silver purse frame
- 18 x 21-inch cotton fabric in color of choice
- Sewing thread to match fabric
- Typing paper

SUPER FINE

## Gauge
12 sts = 2 inches; 14 rnds = 2 inches

## Pattern Notes
Weave in loose ends as work progresses.

Work in continuous rounds; do not turn or join unless otherwise stated.

Mark first stitch of round; move marker up with each round.

Join with slip stitch as indicated unless otherwise stated.

## Purse
**Rnd 1 (RS):** Ch 1, 6 sc in **back bar of ch** (see illustration), **do not join, place marker** (see Pattern Notes). (6 sts)

**Back Bar of Chain**

**Rnd 2:** 2 sc in each st around. (12 sts)

**Rnd 3:** [2 sc in next st, sc in next st] 6 times. (18 sts)

**Rnd 4:** [2 sc in next st, sc in each of next 2 sts] 6 times. (24 sts)

**Rnd 5:** [2 sc in next st, sc in each of next 3 sts] 6 times. (30 sts)

**Rnd 6:** [2 sc in next st, sc in each of next 4 sts] 6 times. (36 sts)

**Rnd 7:** [2 sc in next st, sc in each of next 5 sts] 6 times. (42 sts)

**Rnd 8:** [2 sc in next st, sc in each of next 6 sts] 6 times. (48 sts)

**Rnd 9:** [2 sc in next st, sc in each of next 7 sts] 6 times. (54 sts)

**Rnd 10:** Sc in each st around.

**Rnds 11–23:** Rep rnd 10.

**Rnd 24:** Sc in each st around, **join** (see Pattern Notes) in first sc. Fasten off.

## Lining
Flatten Purse on typing paper as flat as possible then trace around Purse with pencil. Drawing should be about 5 inches wide x 3¾ inches tall. Cut out paper pattern.

Fold fabric in half with RS facing (2 pieces of lining can be cut at the same time), pin paper pattern to material then cut out lining.

With matching thread and holding lining pieces with RS facing, sew a ¼-inch seam around sides and bottom of lining, open top of lining, fold top ¼ inch to WS of material, sew in place. Place lining inside Purse then sew lining in place around Purse opening.

## Finishing
Open purse clasp. With invisible thread, sew purse clasp to Purse opening, sewing an equal number of sts to each side of clasp. ●

# Loves Me, Loves Me Knot Pillowcase Edging

## Materials
- Aunt Lydia's Classic Crochet size 10 crochet cotton (350 yds per ball):
  - 1 ball #856 peacock
- Size 7/1.65mm steel crochet hook or size needed to obtain gauge
- Tapestry needle
- Pillowcase
- Stitch marker

**0 LACE**

## Gauge
5 love knots = 4 inches

## Pattern Notes
When making Back Stitches, do not cut yarn; leave yarn attached to ball.

Weave in loose ends as work progresses.

## Special Stitches
**Love knot:** Pull lp on hook up ¾ inch, yo, pull through lp; sc in back strand of long lp.

**Picot:** Ch 3, insert hook from top to bottom through marked lps, yo, draw through marked lps and lp on hook.

**Single crochet decrease (sc dec):** Insert hook through

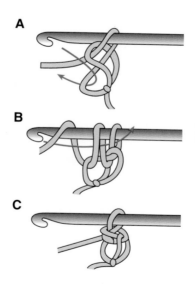

**A**

**B**

**C**

**Love Knot**

## Skill Level
■■□□ EASY

## Finished Measurement
¼ inch wide

end of current back st, yo, draw through, place marker through both lps on hook, keeping marker on front side of fabric, insert hook through beg of next back st, yo, draw through, yo, draw through all 3 lps on hook.

## Edging

### Back Stitches

Thread **yarn** into needle (see Pattern Notes), insert needle in open end edge of pillowcase at seam fold, then working around opening, push needle out to the left ¾ inch from insertion pulling 8 times the length of yarn as the width of the pillowcase through, insert needle ¾ inch to the right in same place as beg insertion then push needle out to the left 1½ inches from insertion pulling yarn through, *insert needle to the right ¾ inch from current location, then push needle out to the left 1½ inches from insertion pulling yarn through, rep from * around opening, adjusting last st as needed to end in same place as beg insertion. Insert needle to the right in same place where next to last st was pulled through, then push needle out to the left in same place as beg back st, pulling rem yarn through.

### Edging

Insert hook through beg of first back st, yo, pull through, ch 1, [sc in current back st, **love knot** (see Special Stitches), **picot** (see Special Stitches)] around to last back st, sc in last back st, love knot, making st same length as last back st, **sc dec** (see Special Stitches), having last leg of dec in beg back st, picot, join with sl st in beg sc. ●

# Thermal Boot Toppers

## Skill Level

■■□□ EASY

## Finished Measurements

13 inches in circumference x 7 inches tall

## Materials

- Plymouth Yarn Encore Worsted Tweed medium (worsted) weight acrylic/wool/rayon yarn (3½ oz/200 yds/100g per skein): 1 skein #6389 ruby
- Sizes H/8/5mm and J/10/6mm crochet hooks or size needed to obtain gauge
- Tapestry needle
- Stitch marker
- ⅝-inch wood buttons: 2 light brown and 2 dark brown
- Measuring tape
- Scissors

## Gauge

**With larger hook:** 11 sts = 4 inches; 14 rows = 4 inches

## Pattern Notes

Weave in loose ends as work progresses.

Join with slip stitch as indicated unless otherwise stated.

Chain-1 at beginning of round does not count as a stitch.

Mark first stitch of round, move marker up with each round.

Work in continuous rounds, do not turn or join unless otherwise stated.

## Special Stitches

**Thermal single crochet-in-front (thermal sc-in-front):** Going from bottom to top, insert hook through unused **front lp** (see Stitch Guide) of st 2 rnds below then through front lp of st on rnd, yo, draw through sts, yo, draw through both lps on hook.

**Thermal single crochet-in-back (thermal sc-in-back):** Insert hook through **back lp** (see Stitch Guide) of st on rnd then going from top to bottom through unused back lp of st 2 rnds below, yo, draw through sts, yo, draw through both lps on hook.

**Closing thermal single crochet-in-front (closing thermal sc-in-front):** Going from bottom to top, insert hook through unused front lp of st 2 rnds below then through both lps of st on rnd, yo, draw through sts, yo, draw through both lps on hook.

## Boot Topper
**Make 2.**

**Rnd 1 (RS):** Leaving 10-inch strand at beg for sewing, with smaller hook, ch 37, sc in **back bar** (see illustration) of 2nd ch from hook and in back bar of each rem ch across, being careful not to twist sts, **join** (see Pattern Notes) in beg sc to form ring. (36 sts)

**Back Bar of Chain**

**Rnd 2: Ch 1** (see Pattern Notes), **fpdc** (see Stitch Guide) around post of same st as beg ch-1, [**bpdc** (see Stitch Guide) around post of next st, fpdc around post of next st] 17 times, bpdc around post of last st, join in beg st.

**Rnds 3 & 4:** [Rep rnd 2] twice.

**Rnd 5:** Ch 1, fpdc around post of st, [bpdc around post of next st, fpdc around post of next st] 17 times, bpdc around post of last st, **do not join** (see Pattern Notes).

**Rnd 6:** With larger hook, sc in back lp of first st, **place marker in st just made** (see Pattern Notes), sc in back lp of each rem st around.

**Rnd 7: Thermal sc-in-front** (see Special Stitches) in each st around.

**Rnd 8: Thermal sc-in-back** (see Special Stitches) in each st around.

**Rnds 9–18:** [Rep rnds 7 and 8] 5 times.

**Rnd 19: Closing thermal sc-in-front** (see Special Stitches) in each st around, join in beg st.

**Rnd 20:** With smaller hook, ch 1, **fpsc** *(see Stitch Guide)* around post of each st around, join in beg st.

**Rnds 21–24:** [Rep rnd 2] 4 times. Fasten off at end of last rnd.

## Finishing

With beg strand, sew bottom of rnd 1 tog. Sew 2 buttons, dark brown above light brown, over rnds 1–5. ●

# Sculpted Basket

## Skill Level
 EASY

## Finished Measurements
8 inches in diameter x 26 inches in circumference x 4 inches tall

## Materials
• Bernat Handicrafter Cotton Stripes medium (worsted) weight cotton yarn (1½ oz/68 yds/ 43g per ball):
    4 balls #4143 country stripes
• Size I/9/5.5mm crochet hook or size needed to obtain gauge
• Tapestry needle
• Stitch marker
• Measuring tape
• Scissors

## Gauge
11 sts = 4 inches; 13 rnds = 4 inches

## Pattern Notes
Weave in loose ends as work progresses.

Pattern is worked with 2 strands of yarn held together throughout.

Mark first stitch of round, move marker up with each round.

Work in continuous rounds, do not turn or join unless otherwise stated.

Join with slip stitch as indicated unless otherwise stated.

## Special Stitches
**Split single crochet (split sc):** Insert hook between legs of next st, yo, draw through st, yo, draw through both lps on hook.

**Split single crochet decrease (split sc dec):** [Insert hook between legs of next st, yo, draw through st] twice, yo, draw through all 3 lps on hook.

## Basket

**Rnd 1 (RS): Holding 2 strands tog** *(see Pattern Notes)*, ch 1, 6 sc in **back bar** *(see illustration)* of ch from hook, **place marker** *(see Pattern Notes)* in first sc made, **do not join** *(see Pattern Notes). (6 sc)*

**Back Bar of Chain**

**Rnd 2:** 2 **split sc** *(see Special Stitches)* in each st around. *(12 sts)*

**Rnd 3:** [2 split sc in next st, split sc in next st] 6 times. *(18 sts)*

**Rnd 4:** [2 split sc in next st, split sc in each of next 2 sts] 6 times. *(24 sts)*

**Rnd 5:** [2 split sc in next st, split sc in each of next 3 sts] 6 times. *(30 sts)*

**Rnd 6:** [2 split sc in next st, split sc in each of next 4 sts] 6 times. *(36 sts)*

**Rnd 7:** [2 split sc in next st, split sc in each of next 5 sts] 6 times. *(42 sts)*

**Rnd 8:** [2 split sc in next st, split sc in each of next 6 sts] 6 times. *(48 sts)*

**Rnd 9:** [2 split sc in next st, split sc in each of next 7 sts] 6 times. *(54 sts)*

**Rnd 10:** [2 split sc in next st, split sc in each of next 8 sts] 6 times. *(60 sts)*

**Rnd 11:** [2 split sc in next st, split sc in each of next 9 sts] 6 times. *(66 sts)*

**Rnd 12:** [2 split sc in next st, split sc in each of next 10 sts] 6 times. *(72 sts)*

**Rnd 13:** Split sc in each st around.

**Rnds 14–20:** [Rep rnd 13] 7 times.

**Rnd 21:** [**Split sc dec** *(see Special Stitches)* over next 2 sts, split sc in each of next 4 sts] 12 times. *(60 sts)*

**Rnd 22:** [Split sc dec over next 2 sts, split sc in each of next 8 sts] 6 times. *(54 sts)*

**Rnd 23:** [2 split sc in next st, split sc in each of next 5 sts] 9 times. *(63 sts)*

**Rnd 24:** [2 split sc in next st, split sc in each of next 6 sts] 9 times. *(72 sts)*

**Rnd 25:** [Sl st in next st, ch 2] 72 times, **join** *(see Pattern Notes)* in beg sl st. Fasten off. *(72 ch-2 sps)* ●

# Tweedy Cables Throw

## Skill Level
 EASY

## Finished Measurements
45 inches wide x 56 inches long

## Materials
- Premier Yarns Mega Tweed super bulky (super chunky) weight acrylic/viscose yarn (6 oz/74 yds/ 170g per ball):
  13 balls #09 burgundy tweed
- Size S/35/19mm crochet hook or size needed to obtain gauge
- Tapestry needle
- Measuring tape
- Scissors

## Gauge

7 sts = 7 inches; 10 rows = 7 inches

## Pattern Notes

Weave in loose ends as work progresses.

All post stitches are worked around post of stitch 2 rows below.

Leave stitch behind post stitch unworked.

Current row is the row you are crocheting. If current row is row 3, then row 2 is one row below and row 1 is two rows below.

## Special Stitches

**Front post double crochet (fpdc):**
Yo, insert hook around post of indicated st 2 rows below from front to back to front, yo, draw through, [yo, draw through 2 lps on hook] twice.

**Closing front post double crochet (closing fpdc):** Yo, insert hook around post of last st 2 rows below from front to back to front, yo, draw through, yo, draw through 2 lps on hook, insert hook through turning ch 1 row below, yo, draw through, yo, draw through all 3 lps on hook.

**Front post treble crochet (fptr):** Yo twice, insert hook around post of indicated post st 2 rows below from front to back to front, yo, draw through, [yo, draw through 2 lps on hook] 3 times.

**Front post treble cross (fptr cross):** Sk next post st, **fptr** (see Special Stitches) around post of next post st, sc in sc st, fptr around post of sk post st.

## Throw

**Row 1 (RS):** Ch 48, sc in **back bar** (see illustration) of 2nd ch from hook (sk ch counts as turning ch), sc in back bar of each rem ch across, turn. (47 sts)

**Back Bar of Chain**

**Row 2:** Ch 1, sc in each st across to last st, sk last st, sc in turning ch, turn.

**Row 3:** Ch 1, **fpdc** (see Special Stitches) around post of first st **2 rows below** (see Pattern Notes), [sc in each of next 3 sts, fpdc around post of next st 2 rows below, sc in next st, fpdc around post of next st 2 rows below] 7 times, sc in each of next 3 sts, **closing fpdc** (see Special Stitches) around post of last st 2 rows below, turn.

**Row 4:** Ch 1, sc in each st across to last st, sk last st, sc in turning ch, turn.

**Row 5:** Ch 1, fpdc around post of first post st, [sc in each of next 3 sts, fpdc around post of next post st, sc in next st, fpdc around post of next post st] 7 times, sc in each of next 3 sts, closing fpdc around post of last post st, turn.

**Row 6:** Ch 1, sc in each st across to last st, sk last st, sc in turning ch, turn.

**Row 7:** Ch 1, fpdc around post of first post st, [sc in each of next 3 sts, **fptr cross** *(see Special Stitches)*] 7 times, sc in each of next 3 sts, closing fpdc around post of last post st, turn.

**Rows 8–15:** [Rep rows 4 and 5] 4 times.

**Rows 16 & 17:** [Rep rows 6 and 7] once.

**Rows 18–25:** [Rep rows 4–7] twice.

**Rows 26–33:** [Rep rows 4 and 5] 4 times.

**Rows 34 & 35:** [Rep rows 6 and 7] once.

**Rows 36–39:** [Rep rows 4 and 5] twice.

**Rows 40 & 41:** [Rep rows 6 and 7] once.

**Rows 42–45:** [Rep rows 4 and 5] twice.

**Rows 46 & 47:** [Rep rows 6 and 7] once.

**Rows 48–55:** [Rep rows 4 and 5] 4 times.

**Rows 56 & 57:** [Rep rows 6 and 7] once.

**Rows 58–65:** [Rep rows 4–7] twice.

**Rows 66–73:** [Rep rows 4 and 5] 4 times.

**Rows 74 & 75:** [Rep rows 6 and 7] once.

**Rows 76–79:** [Rep rows 4 and 5] twice.

**Row 80:** Rep row 4. Fasten off. ●

# Country Angel

## Skill Level
■ ■ □ □ EASY

## Finished Measurement
2½ inches tall

## Gauge
10 sts = 1 inch; 9 rows = 1 inch

## Pattern Notes
Weave in loose ends as work progresses.

Join with slip stitch as indicated unless otherwise stated.

Mark first stitch of round, move marker up with each round.

## Materials
- Aunt Lydia's Classic Crochet size 10 crochet cotton (natural and white: 400 yds per ball; solids: 350 yds per ball):
    1 ball each #226 natural, #01 white and #493 French rose
- Size 7/1.65mm steel crochet hook or size needed to obtain gauge
- Tapestry needle
- 5 stitch markers
- 1⅛ x 1⅝-inch Woodpile Fun! birch egg
- 20mm round wood natural bead
- 20mm rusty gold shank button
- Floral baby's breath
- Grass heather stem
- Self-sealing floral tape
- Clear drying craft glue
- Fabric stiffener
- Waxed dental floss
- Measuring tape
- Scissors

**0 LACE**

Work in continuous rounds, do not turn or join unless otherwise stated.

Chain-3 at beginning of row does not count as a stitch.

## Dress

**Rnd 1 (RS):** With French rose, leaving 10-inch strand at beg for sewing, ch 15, sc in **back bar** *(see illustration)* of 2nd ch from hook *(place marker in front lp of last st for Collar placement)*, sc in back bar of each rem ch across, being careful not to twist sts, **join** *(see Pattern Notes)* in **back lp** *(see Stitch Guide)* of beg sc to form ring. *(14 sc)*

**Back Bar of Chain**

**Rnd 2:** Ch 1, sc in same back lp as beg ch-1, **place marker in sc just made** *(see Pattern Notes)*, [ch 1, sc in back lp of next st] 13 times, **do not join** *(see Pattern Notes)*. *(27 sts)*

**Rnd 3:** [Ch 1, sk sc, sc in ch-1 sp] 3 times, *ch 3 *(for armhole)*, sk (sc, ch 1, sc), sc in next ch-1 sp*, [ch 1, sk next sc, sc in next ch-1 sp] 4 times, rep from * to * once, [ch 1, sk next sc, sc in next ch-1 sp] 2 times, ch 1, sk last sc.

**Rnd 4:** [Sc in ch-1 sp, ch 1, sk next sc] 3 times, *(sc, ch 1, sc) in ch-3 sp*, [ch 1, sk next sc, sc in next ch-1 sp] 4 times, ch 1, sk next sc, rep from * to * once, [ch 1, sk next sc, sc in next ch-1 sp] 3 times.

**Rnd 5:** [Ch 1, sk next sc, sc in next ch-1 sp] 13 times, ch 1, sk last sc, join in beg ch-1 sp. Fasten off.

With beg strand, sew bottom of rnd 1 tog.

## Pinafore Skirt

**Rnd 1:** With RS facing, join white in beg ch-1 sp on Dress rnd 5, ch 1, sc in same ch-1 sp as joining, sc in next sc, sc in next ch-1 sp, sc in next sc *(place marker*

*in front lp of last st for first strap placement)*, [sc in next ch-1 sp, sc in next sc] 7 times *(place marker in front lp of last st for Pinafore Bib placement)*, [sc in next ch-1 sp, sc in next sc] 3 times *(place marker in front lp of last st for second strap placement)*, sc in next ch-1 sp, sc in next sc, sc in last sp, do not join. *(27 sts)*

**Rnd 2:** Sc in back lp of first sc, [ch 2, sk next sc, sc in back lp of next sc] 13 times. *(40 sts)*

**Rnd 3:** [Ch 2, sk next sc, sc in next ch-2 sp] 13 times, ch 2, sk last sc. *(41 sts)*

**Rnd 4:** Sc in ch-2 sp, [ch 2, sk next sc, sc in next ch-2 sp] 13 times. *(40 sts)*

**Rnds 5 & 6:** [Rep rnds 3 and 4] once.

**Rnd 7:** [Ch 2, sk next sc, sc in next ch-2 sp] 13 times, ch 1, sk last sc. *(40 sts)*

**Rnd 8:** Sl st in **front lp** *(see Stitch Guide)* of each ch and st around, join in beg sl st. Fasten off.

## Dress Ruffle

**Rnd 1:** With RS facing, join French rose to Pinafore Skirt rnd 7 in unused back lp on back of skirt, ch 1, (sc, ch 2, dc) in same lp as joining, [sk next back lp, (sc, ch 2, dc) in next back lp] 19 times, sk last back lp, join in beg st. Fasten off. *(20 [sc, ch 2, dc] groups)*

## Sleeve
**Make 2.**

**Rnd 1 (RS):** Join French rose to armhole opening, ch 1, sc in same sp as joining, [ch 1, sc] 5 times evenly sp around opening, do not join. *(11 sts)*

**Rnd 2:** [Ch 1, sk next sc, sc in ch-1 sp] 5 times, ch 1, sk last sc.

**Rnd 3:** [Sc in ch-1 sp, ch 1, sk next sc] 5 times, sc in last ch-1 sp.

**Rnds 4–7:** [Rep rnds 2 and 3] twice.

**Rnd 8:** [Ch 1, sk next sc, sc in ch-1 sp] 5 times, ch 1, sk last sc, join in beg st. Fasten off, leaving long end for sewing.

## Hand
**Make 2.**

With natural, ch 6, sc in back bar of 2nd ch from hook and in back bar of each rem ch across. Fasten off. *(5 sts)*

Push Hand inside Sleeve opening, leaving ¼ inch of hand showing. Weave long strand on Sleeve through ch-1 sps on Sleeve rnd 8. Pull tight to close sleeve around hand; sew in place.

## Pinafore Bib

**Row 1 (RS):** With RS facing and Dress RS up, join white in marked lp for pinafore bib placement, ch 1, sc in same lp as joining, sc in unused front lp of each of next 8 sts, turn. *(9 sts)*

**Row 2:** Ch 1, **sc dec** *(see Stitch Guide)* over first 2 sts, sc in each of next 5 sts, sc dec over last 2 sts, turn. *(7 sts)*

**Row 3:** Ch 1, sc in first st *(place marker in last st made)*, sc in each st across, ch 10, going over shoulder, join in marked st for first strap placement. Fasten off.

## 2nd Strap

Join white in marked st on row 3, ch 10, going over shoulder, join in marked st for 2nd strap placement. Fasten off.

## Collar

With RS facing and Dress upside down, join French rose in marked lp for collar placement, ch 1, sc in same lp as joining, working in unused front lps around, sc in each of next 2 lps, [ch 1, hdc in next lp] twice, [ch 1, dc in next lp] twice, ch 2, sl st in same lp as last dc, sl st in next lp, ch 2, dc in same lp as last sl st, ch 1, dc in next lp, [ch 1, hdc in next lp] twice, ch 1, sc in each of last 3 lps. Fasten off.

## Heart

With French rose, ch 5, (sl st, ch 4, sl st) in 5th ch from hook, ch 1, join in 2nd ch of beg ch-5. Fasten off, leaving long end for sewing.

Sew Heart to center of Bib.

## Wings

**Row 1 (RS):** With white, ch 11, sc in 2nd ch from hook, [ch 2, sk next 2 chs, sc in next ch] 3 times, turn. *(10 sts)*

**Row 2:** Ch 3 *(see Pattern Notes)*, sc in 2nd ch from hook, ch 2, sk next ch and sc, sc in next ch-2 sp, [ch 2, sk next sc, sc in next ch-2 sp] twice, ch 2, sk last sc, sc in beg ch-1, turn. *(13 sts)*

**Row 3:** Ch 3, sc in 2nd ch from hook, ch 2, sk next ch and sc, sc in next ch-2 sp, [ch 2, sk next sc, sc in next ch-2 sp] 3 times, ch 2, sk last sc, sc in beg ch-1, turn. *(16 sts)*

**Row 4:** Ch 3, sc in 2nd ch from hook, ch 2, sk next ch and sc, sc in next ch-2 sp, [ch 2, sk next sc, sc in next ch-2 sp] 3 times, turn, leaving rem 4 sts unworked. *(13 sts)*

**Row 5:** Ch 1, sk sc, sc in ch-2 sp, [ch 2, sk next sc, sc in next ch-2 sp] 3 times, ch 2, sk last sc, sc in beg ch-1, turn. *(13 sts)*

**Row 6:** Ch 3, sc in 2nd ch from hook, ch 2, sk next ch and sc, sc in next ch-2 sp, [ch 2, sk next sc, sc in next ch-2 sp] twice, turn, leaving rem 4 sts unworked. *(10 sts)*

**Row 7:** Ch 1, sk first sc, sc in next ch-2 sp, [ch 2, sk next sc, sc in next ch-2 sp] twice, ch 2, sk last sc, sc in beg ch-1, turn to work across ends of rows. *(10 sts)*

**Row 8:** Ch 2, sk end of first row, sc in end of next row, [ch 2, sc in end of next row] 3 times *(place marker in last ch-2 sp for joining placement)*, [ch 2, sc in end of next row] twice, do not turn, do not fasten off. *(18 sts)*

**Rows 9–15:** [Rep rows 1–7] once.

**Row 16:** Ch 2, sk end of first row, sc in end of next row, [ch 2, sc in end of next row] 3 times, ch 2,

join in marked st on row 8. Fasten off, leaving long end for sewing. *(14 sts)*

Sew Wings to back of Dress.

## Finishing

Cut 2 sprigs grass ¾-inch long and 2 heather flowers with stems ¾-inch long from grass heather stem. Cut one baby's breath flower with stem ¾ inch long. Holding flowers and grass tog, wrap self-sealing floral tape around stems and grass to form bouquet.

Arrange right arm to hold miniature bouquet; sew in place. Arrange left arm as desired; sew in place.

Glue bodice of Dress over egg/body. Glue bead/head on top of body; glue button/halo on top of head.

Place small amount of fabric stiffener on Wings; shape as desired. ●

# Gingham Dishcloths

### Skill Level
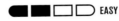 **EASY**

### Finished Measurement
7½ inches square

### Gauge
12 sts = 4 inches; 14 rows = 4 inches

## Materials

- Bernat Handicrafter Cotton medium (worsted) weight cotton yarn (1¾ oz/80 yds/50g per ball):
    - 1 ball each #1001 white and #2746 summer prints
- Bernat Handicrafter Cotton Stripes medium (worsted) weight cotton yarn (1½ oz/68 yds/43g per ball):
    - 1 ball #4143 country stripes
- Size H/8/5mm crochet hook or size needed to obtain gauge
- Tapestry needle
- Measuring tape
- Scissors

**4 MEDIUM**

## Pattern Notes

Weave in loose ends as work progresses.

Two colors of yarn are used on each row (one at a time), when instructed to work over yarn, place color not being used on wrong side of fabric then crochet over it; when not instructed to work over yarn, drop color not being used to wrong side of fabric.

Work in continuous rounds; do not turn or join unless otherwise stated.

Join with slip stitch as indicated unless otherwise stated.

## Country Edging Gingham Dishcloth

*Note: Rows 1–8 are crocheted with summer print and country stripes.*

**Row 1 (RS):** With summer print, ch 21, ch 1, **change color** (*see Stitch Guide*) to country stripes, **working over summer print** (*see Pattern Notes*), sc in 2nd ch from hook and in each of next 5 chs, sc in next ch, changing to summer print, working over country stripes, sc in each of next 6 chs, sc in next ch, changing to country stripes, sc in each of last 7 chs, turn. (*21 sc*)

**Row 2:** Ch 1, sc in each of first 6 sts, sc in next st, changing to summer print, sc in next st, working over country stripes, sc in each of next 5 sts, sc in next st, changing to country stripes, sc in each of last 7 sts, turn.

**Row 3:** Ch 1, sc in each of first 6 sts, sc in next st, changing to summer print, working over country stripes, sc in each of next 6 sts, sc in next st, changing to country stripes, sc in each of last 7 sts, turn.

**Rows 4–7:** [Rep rows 2 and 3] twice.

**Row 8:** Ch 1, sc in each of first 6 sts, sc in next st, changing to summer print, sc in next st, working over country stripes, sc in each of next 5 sts, sc in next st, changing to country stripes, sc in next st, working over summer print, sc in each of next 5 sts, sc in last st, changing to summer print, turn. Fasten off country stripes.

*Note: Rows 9–16 are crocheted with summer print and white.*

**Row 9:** Ch 1, sc in each of first 6 sts, sc in next st, changing to white, working over summer print, sc in each of next 6 sts, sc in next st, changing to summer print, sc in each of last 7 sts, turn.

**Row 10:** Ch 1, sc in each of first 6 sts, sc in next st, changing to white, sc in next st, working over summer print, sc in each of next 5 sts, sc in next st, changing to summer print, sc in each of last 7 sts, turn.

**Rows 11–14:** [Rep rows 9 and 10] twice.

**Row 15:** Rep row 9.

**Row 16:** Ch 1, sc in each of first 6 sts, sc in next st, changing to white, sc in next st, working over summer print, sc in each of next 5 sts, sc in next st, changing to summer print, sc in each of next 6 sts, sc in last st, changing to country stripes, turn. Fasten off white.

*Note: Rows 17–24 are crocheted with summer print and country stripes.*

**Row 17:** Ch 1, working over summer print, sc in each of first 6 sts, sc in next st, changing to summer print, working over country stripes, sc in each of next 6 sts, sc in next st, changing to country stripes, sc in each of last 7 sts, turn.

**Rows 18–23:** [Rep rows 2 and 3] 3 times.

**Row 24:** Rep row 2. Fasten off country stripes and summer print.

## Edging

**Rnd 1 (RS):** With RS facing, **join** (see Pattern Notes) white in last st, ch 1, sc in same st as joining and in each st across, *ch 1 (for corner), turn to work across ends of rows, evenly sp 21 sc across ends of rows, ch 1 (for corner)*, turn to work across beg ch, sc in each unused lp of foundation ch, rep from * to * once, **do not join** (see Pattern Notes). (84 sc, 4 ch-1 corner sps)

**Rnd 2:** Sl st in each st and ch-1 sp around, join in beg sl st. Fasten off. (88 sl sts)

## White Edging Gingham Dishcloth
Work same as Country Edging Gingham Dishcloth working all country stripes sts with white and all white sts with country stripes. ●

# Rolled Brim 18" Doll Hat

## Skill Level
 EASY

## Finished Measurements
11 inches in circumference (not including brim) x 4¾ inches tall

## Materials
- Premier Yarns Deborah Norville Everyday Soft medium (worsted) weight acrylic yarn (4 oz/203 yds/ 113g per skein):
    1 skein each #32 peony and #27 lemon
- Size H/8/5mm crochet hook or size needed to obtain gauge
- Tapestry needle
- Stitch markers: 2
- Measuring tape
- Scissors

## Gauge
13 sts = 4 inches; 15 rows = 4 inches

## Pattern Notes

Weave in loose ends as work progresses.

Mark first stitch of round, move marker up with each round.

Work in continuous rounds, do not turn or join unless otherwise stated.

Join with slip stitch as indicated unless otherwise stated.

## Special Stitch

**French knot:** Attach strand to back of flower, bring needle from back of fabric to front of fabric through center of flower, keeping strand taut, wrap yarn 5 times around needle then push needle from front of fabric to back of fabric near center of flower catching a flower thread so that knot stays on front of flower.

## Hat

**Rnd 1 (RS):** With peony, ch 1, 6 sc in **back bar of ch** (see illustration), **place marker** in first sc made (see Pattern Notes), **do not join** (see Pattern Notes). (6 sts)

**Back Bar of Chain**

**Rnd 2:** 2 sc in each st around. (12 sts)

**Rnd 3:** [2 sc in st, sc in next st] 6 times. (18 sts)

**Rnd 4:** [2 sc in st, sc in each of next 2 sts] 6 times. (24 sts)

**Rnd 5:** [2 sc in st, sc in each of next 3 sts] 6 times. (30 sts)

**Rnd 6:** [2 sc in st, sc in each of next 4 sts] 6 times. (36 sts)

**Rnd 7:** Sc in each st around.

**Rnds 8–13:** [Rep rnd 7] 6 times.

**Rnd 14:** Sc in each st around, **join** (see Pattern Notes) in beg st.

**Rnd 15:** Ch 1, sc in same st as beg ch-1, *ch 1, sk next st, sc in next st, rep from * around to last st, ch 1, sk last st, join in beg sc. (18 ch-1 sps)

**Rnd 16:** Ch 1, sc, *sc in ch-1 sp, sc in next st, rep from * around to last ch-1 sp, sc in last ch-1 sp, do not join. (36 sts)

**Rnd 17:** *Sl st in **front lp** (see Stitch Guide) of st then sl st in **back lp** (see Stitch Guide) of same st, rep from * around, do not join. (72 sts)

**Rnd 18:** Sl st in front lp of each st around.

**Rnds 19–21:** [Rep rnd 18] 3 times. Fasten off at end of last rnd.

## Hat Band

Cut 2 20-inch strands of lemon. Holding both strands tog, weave strands through ch-1 sps of rnd 15 of Hat. Tie ends tog. Fasten off excess yarn.

## Flower

**Rnd 1 (RS):** With lemon, ch 5, sl st in 5th ch from hook, [ch 4, sl st in same ch as beg sl st] 4 times, do not join. (5 ch-4 sps)

**Rnd 2:** [Sl st in ch-4 sp, ch 1, (sc, 2 dc, sc, sl st) in same ch-4 sp as last sl st] 5 times, join in beg sl st. Fasten off, leaving long strand for sewing.

Cut 12-inch strand of peony. With peony strand and tapestry needle, make **French knot** (see Special Stitch) in center of Flower.

## Finishing

With long lemon strand, sew Flower over hat band knot. ●

# 18" Doll Scarf

## Skill Level
■■□□ EASY

## Finished Measurements
1½ inches wide x 13 inches long

## Materials
- Premier Yarns Deborah Norville Everyday Soft medium (worsted) weight acrylic yarn (4 oz/203 yds/ 113g per skein):
    1 skein each #32 peony and #27 lemon
- Size H/8/5mm crochet hook or size needed to obtain gauge
- Tapestry needle
- Stitch markers: 2
- Measuring tape
- Scissors

## Gauge
13 sts = 4 inches; 15 rows = 4 inches

## Pattern Notes
Weave in loose ends as work progresses.

Join with slip stitch as indicated unless otherwise stated.

## Scarf
**Row 1 (RS):** With peony, ch 52, sc in **back bar** (see illustration) of 2nd ch from hook and in back bar of each rem ch across, turn. (51 sts)

**Back Bar of Chain**

**Row 2:** Ch 1, sc in same st as beg ch-1, *ch 1, sk next st, sc in next st, rep from * across (place marker in last ch-1 sp), turn. (25 ch-1 sps)

**Row 3:** Ch 1, sc in each st and ch-1 sp across, turn. (51 sts)

**Rows 4 & 5:** [Rep rows 2 and 3] once. Fasten off at end of last row, leaving long end for sewing.

## Scarf Band
Cut 2 40-inch strands of lemon. With RS facing and holding both strands tog, join strands to scarf by pulling 20 inches of yarn from front to back through marked ch-1 sp on row 2 then from back to front through marked ch-1 sp on row 4. Weave beg of strands through ch-1 sps on row 2 then weave end of strands through ch-1 sps on row 4. Tie ends tog on WS of work. Fasten off excess yarn.

With RS facing, fold end of Scarf with scarf band knot back forming 2-inch lp. With long strand, sew in place across ends of rows 1–5. ●

# Decorative Cards

## Balloons Aloft Greeting Card

### Skill Level

 EASY

### Finished Measurements

5½ inches wide x 4 inches long

### Gauge

Balloon = 1¼ inches tall

### Pattern Notes

Weave in loose ends as work progresses.

Join with slip stitch as indicated unless otherwise stated.

Chain-3 at beginning of round counts as first double crochet unless otherwise stated.

### Special Stitch

**Beginning double crochet decrease (beg dc dec):** Ch 2, dc in next st.

### Materials

- Aunt Lydia's Classic Crochet size 10 crochet cotton (350 yds per ball):
  1 ball each #421 goldenrod, #451 parakeet and #493 French rose
- Size 7/1.65mm steel crochet hook or size needed to obtain gauge
- Tapestry needle
- 5½-inch x 4-inch blank greeting card
- 1½-inch-wide burlap ribbon: 5½ inches
- ⅝-inch-wide ribbon in color of choice: 7½ inches
- Word stamps and ink in color of choice
- Clear drying craft glue
- Measuring tape
- Scissors

### Balloon

**Make 1 in each color.**

**Rnd 1 (RS):** Ch 4, 11 dc in 4th ch from hook *(3 sk chs count as a dc)*, **join** *(see Pattern Notes)* in top of beg ch-4. *(12 sts)*

**Rnd 2:** Ch 3 *(see Pattern Notes)*, dc in same st as beg ch-3, 2 dc in each st around, join in top of beg ch-3. *(24 sts)*

**Rnd 3:** Ch 3, dc in each st around, join in top of beg ch-3.

**Rnd 4:** Beg dc dec *(see Special Stitches)* over first 2 sts, [**dc dec** *(see Stitch Guide)* over next 2 sts] 11 times, join in top of beg dc dec st. *(12 sts)*

**Rnd 5:** Beg dc dec over first 2 sts, [dc dec over next 2 sts] 5 times, join in top of beg dc dec st. *(6 sts)*

**Rnd 6:** Ch 3, **sc dec** *(see Stitch Guide)* over first 2 sts, [ch 3, sc dec over next 2 sts] twice, join in same st as beg ch-3. Fasten off leaving 5-inch strand for balloon string. *(3 ch-3 sps)*

## Assembly

Wrap balloon string strand tightly around Balloon between rnds 5 and 6 three times to create Balloon tie; then pull end of Balloon string through tie to lock in place. Trim string as desired.

## Finishing

Using photo as guide, glue center 5½ inches of ribbon across middle of burlap. Fold 1 inch of ribbon under on each end; glue ends in place. Glue ribbon/burlap to card. Glue Balloons on top of ribbon; stamp message of choice.

## Sunflowers Greeting Card

### Skill Level
 EASY

### Finished Measurements
5½ inches wide x 4 inches long

### Gauge
Sunflower = 1½ inches in diameter

### Pattern Notes
Weave in loose ends as work progresses.

Join with slip stitch as indicated unless otherwise stated.

Chain-3 at beginning of round counts as first double crochet unless otherwise stated.

## Materials
- Aunt Lydia's Classic Crochet size 10 crochet cotton (350 yds per ball):
    1 ball each #131 fudge brown, #421 goldenrod and #484 myrtle green
- Size 7/1.65mm steel crochet hook or size needed to obtain gauge
- Tapestry needle
- 5½-inch x 4-inch blank greeting card
- ⅜-inch-wide ribbon in color of choice: 6 inches
- Word stamps and ink in color of choice
- Clear drying craft glue
- Measuring tape
- Scissors

### Sunflower
**Make 3.**

**Rnd 1 (RS):** With fudge brown, ch 4, 11 dc in 4th ch from hook *(3 sk chs count as a dc)*, **join** *(see Pattern Notes)* in top of beg ch-4. *(12 sts)*

**Rnd 2:** Ch 3 *(see Pattern Notes)*, **fptr** *(see Stitch Guide)* around post of same st as beg ch-3, [dc in next st, fptr around post of same st as last dc] 11 times, join in top of beg ch-3. Fasten off. *(24 sts)*

**Rnd 3:** Join goldenrod in any st, [ch 5, sl st in next st] 24 times *(last sl st will be in same st as beg ch-5)*. Fasten off. *(24 ch-5 sps)*

## Leaf
**Make 3.**

With myrtle green, leaving 10-inch strand at beg for stem, ch 12, sc in 2nd ch from hook, hdc in next ch, dc in each of next 2 chs, tr in each of next 2 chs, dc in each of next 2 chs, hdc in next ch, sc in next ch, sl st in last ch, working on opposite side of foundation ch in unused lps, sk ch where sl st was made, sc in unused lp of ch where last sc was made, hdc in next unused lp, dc in each of next 2 unused lps, tr in each of next 2 unused lps, dc in each of next 2 unused lps, hdc in next unused lp, sc in last unused lp, join in beg sc. Fasten off. *(21 sts)*

## Finishing
Using photo as guide, glue Leaves and Sunflowers on card. Fold 1 inch of ribbon under on each end. Glue ends in place. Glue ribbon on card; stamp message of choice. ●

# Dolly's Spring Jumper

## Skill Level
 EASY

## Finished Size
Fits 18-inch doll with 10¼-inch chest circumference and 12-inch hip circumference

## Gauge
13 sts = 4 inches; 15 rows = 4 inches

## Pattern Notes
Weave in loose ends as work progresses.

Join with slip stitch as indicated unless otherwise stated.

## Special Stitches
**Beginning double crochet decrease (beg dc dec):** With RS facing, join yarn in st, ch 2, dc in next st.

## Materials
- Premier Yarns Ever Soft medium (worsted) weight acrylic yarn (3 oz/158 yds/85g per skein):
  1 skein each #02 sunflower, #20 dark teal and #36 white
- Size H/8/5mm crochet hook or size needed to obtain gauge
- Tapestry needle
- Sewing needle
- Stitch marker
- 20mm shank buttons: 2 daisy buttons
- 9mm sew-on snaps: 2 snaps
- Matching dark teal sewing thread
- Measuring tape
- Scissors

**Beginning split double crochet decrease (beg split dc dec):** With RS facing, join yarn in sp between first leg and 2nd leg of a dec st, ch 2, dc in sp between first leg and 2nd leg of next dec st.

**Split double crochet decrease (split dc dec):** Yo, insert hook in same sp as last leg of last dec st, yo, draw through sp, yo, draw through 2 lps on hook, yo, insert hook in sp between first leg and 2nd leg of next dec st, yo, draw through sp, yo, draw through 2 lps on hook, yo, draw through all 3 lps on hook.

# Jumper

## Skirt

**Rnd 1 (RS):** With dark teal, leaving 10-inch strand at beg for sewing, ch 37, sc in **back bar** *(see illustration)* of 2nd ch from hook and in back bar of each of next 28 chs *(place marker in unused lps of ch where last sc was made to mark bib placement)*, sc in back bar of each of last 7 chs, being careful not to twist sts, **join** *(see Pattern Notes)* in beg sc to form ring. Fasten off. *(36 sts)*

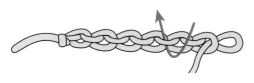

**Back Bar of Chain**

With beg strand, sew bottom of rnd 1 tog.

**Rnd 2:** With white, **beg dc dec** *(see Special Stitches)* over first 2 sts, [ch 1, **dc dec** *(see Stitch Guide)* over next 2 sts] 17 times, ch 1, join in top of beg dc dec. Fasten off. *(18 dec sts)*

**Rnd 3:** With dark teal, **beg split dc dec** *(see Special Stitches)*, [ch 1, **split dc dec** *(see Special Stitches)*] 17 times *(last leg of last split dc dec will be in same sp as beg ch-2)*, ch 1, join in top of beg split dc dec. Fasten off.

**Rnd 4:** With white, beg split dc dec, [ch 1, split dc dec] 17 times *(last leg of last split dc dec will be in same sp as beg ch-2)*, ch 1, join in top of beg split dc dec.

**Rnd 5:** Ch 1, [2 sc in st, sc in ch-1 sp, sc in next st, 2 sc in ch-1 sp, sc in next st, sc in ch-1 sp] 6 times, join in beg sc. Fasten off. *(48 sts)*

**Rnd 6:** With dark teal, beg dc dec over first 2 sts, [ch 1, dc dec over next 2 sts] 23 times, ch 1, join in top of beg dc dec. Fasten off. *(24 dec sts)*

**Rnd 7:** With sunflower, beg split dc dec, [ch 1, split dc dec] 23 times *(last leg of last split dc dec will be in same sp as beg ch-2)*, ch 1, join in top of beg split dc dec. Fasten off.

**Rnd 8:** With dark teal, beg split dc dec, [ch 1, split dc dec] 23 times *(last leg of last split dc dec will be in same sp as beg ch-2)*, ch 1, join in top of beg split dc dec.

**Rnd 9:** Ch 1, [2 sc in st, sc in ch-1 sp, sc in next st, sc in next ch-1 sp] 12 times, join in beg sc. Fasten off. *(60 sts)*

**Rnd 10:** With sunflower, beg dc dec over first 2 sts, [ch 1, dc dec over next 2 sts] 29 times, ch 1, join in top of beg dc dec. Fasten off. *(30 dec sts)*

**Rnd 11:** With white, beg split dc dec, [ch 1, split dc dec] 29 times *(last leg of last split dc dec will be in same sp as beg ch-2)*, ch 1, join in top of beg split dc dec. Fasten off.

**Rnd 12:** With sunflower, beg split dc dec, [ch 1, split dc dec] 29 times *(last leg of last split dc dec will be in same sp as beg ch-2)*, ch 1, join in top of beg split dc dec.

**Rnd 13:** Ch 1, *2 sc in st, [sc in next ch-1 sp, sc in next st] twice, 2 sc in next ch-1 sp, [sc in next st, sc in next ch-1 sp] twice, rep from * 5 times, join in beg sc. Fasten off. *(72 sts)*

## Bib

**Row 1 (RS):** With RS facing, join dark teal in marked lps for bib placement, ch 1, sc in same lps as joining, working in unused lps of foundation ch, sc in each of next 21 unused lps, turn. *(22 sts)*

**Row 2:** Ch 1, **sc dec** *(see Stitch Guide)* over first 2 sts, sc in each of next 18 sts, sc dec over last 2 sts, turn. *(20 sts)*

**Row 3:** Ch 1, sc dec over first 2 sts, sc in each of next 16 sts, sc dec over last 2 sts, turn. *(18 sts)*

**Row 4:** Ch 1, sc dec over first 2 sts, sc in each of next 14 sts, sc dec over last 2 sts, turn. *(16 sts)*

**Row 5:** Ch 1, sc dec over first 2 sts, sc in each of next 12 sts, sc dec over last 2 sts, turn. *(14 sts)*

**Row 6:** Ch 1, sc in each st across, turn.

**Rows 7 & 8:** [Rep row 6] twice. Fasten off at end of last row.

## Strap

### First Strap

**Row 1:** With RS facing, join dark teal in next unused lp of foundation ch, ch 1, sc in same lp as joining, working in unused lps across, sc in each of next 4 unused lps *(place marker in last sc for 2nd strap placement)*, sc in each of last 9 unused lps, turn. *(14 sts)*

**Row 2:** Ch 1, sc dec over first 2 sts, sc in next st, sc dec over next 2 sts, turn leaving rem sts unworked. *(3 sts)*

**Row 3:** Ch 1, sc in each st across, turn.

**Rows 4–25:** [Rep row 3] 22 times. Fasten off at end of last row.

### 2nd Strap

**Row 1:** With WS facing, join dark teal in marked st for second strap placement, ch 1, sc dec over first 2 sts, sc in next st, sc dec over last 2 sts, turn. *(3 sts)*

**Row 2:** Ch 1, sc in each st across, turn.

**Rows 3–24:** [Rep row 2] 22 times. Do not turn at end of last row.

### Edging

With RS facing and with dark teal, sl st evenly sp around Jumper opening, join in beg sl st. Fasten off.

### Finishing

With RS facing, sew shank button to end of each shoulder strap, then with WS facing, sew socket half of sew-on snap to each shoulder strap directly behind button.

Sew ball half of 2 sew-on snaps to Bib between rows 7 and 8 so that snaps are centered 2½ inches apart. ●

# Ruby Beaded Ring

## Skill Level
 EASY

## Finished Measurement
¾ inch in diameter

## Materials
- Aunt Lydia's Classic Crochet size 10 crochet cotton (350 yds per ball):
  - 1 ball #196 cardinal
- Size 7/1.65mm steel crochet hook or size needed to obtain gauge
- Tapestry needle
- Stitch marker
- 6/0 transparent seed beads: 33 dark red
- The Jewelry Shoppe findings adjustable ring with 12mm pad
- Clear drying craft glue
- Waxed dental floss
- Scissors

## Gauge
5 bead sc = 1 inch

## Pattern Notes
Weave in loose ends as work progresses.

Mark first stitch of round, move marker up with each round.

Work in continuous rounds, do not turn or join unless otherwise stated.

## Special Stitch
**Bead single crochet (bead sc):** Push bead up to hook, sc in indicated st. Bead will appear on back (RS) of fabric.

## Ring

### Beading Needle
To make beading needle, cut 8-inch piece of waxed dental floss. Hold ends of floss tog forming lp (eye of needle). Squeeze ends of floss tog so that they stick tog forming point of needle.

**Rnd 1 (WS):** With beading needle, string 33 beads onto thread, ch 1, 6 sc in **back bar** (see illustration) of ch, **do not join** (see Pattern Notes). (6 sts)

**Back Bar of Chain**

**Rnd 2:** 2 sc in each st around. (12 sts)

**Rnd 3:** Bead sc (see Special Stitch) in each st around.

**Rnd 4:** Rep rnd 3.

**Rnd 5:** [Sk next st, bead sc in next st] 6 times. *(6 sts)*

**Rnd 6:** [Sk next st, bead sc in next st] 3 times. Fasten off. *(3 sts)*

## Finishing
Push cut strand through center of rnd 1; pull tight to close. Glue rnds 1 and 2 to pad of ring. ●

# Root Beer Post Scarf for Him

## Skill Level
 EASY

## Finished Measurements
6 inches wide x 71 inches long, excluding fringe

## Materials
- Premier Yarns Sweet Roll medium (worsted) weight acrylic yarn (5 oz/245 yds/140g per ball):
  2 balls #25 root beer pop
- Size J/10/6mm crochet hook or size needed to obtain gauge
- Tapestry needle
- Measuring tape
- Scissors

## Gauge
14 sts = 5 inches; 6 rows = 4 inches

## Pattern Notes
Weave in loose ends as work progresses.

Chain-3 at beginning of row counts as first double crochet unless otherwise stated.

## Special Stitches
**Post puff:** [Yo, insert hook from front to back to front around post of dc just made, yo, draw through] twice, yo, draw through all 5 lps on hook.

**Lark's Head Knot:** Hold 2 matching color strands tog, fold in half, with WS facing insert hook in end of row, place center of strands on hook and draw through, wrap ends of strands over hook, draw through lp on hook, pull ends to tighten.

## Scarf

**Row 1 (RS):** Ch 188, dc in **back bar** (see illustration) of 4th ch from hook (3 sk chs count as a dc), dc in back bar of each rem ch across, turn. (186 dc)

**Back Bar of Chain**

**Row 2: Ch 3** (see Pattern Notes), [dc in next st, **post puff** (see Special Stitches), sk next st] across to last st, dc in last st, turn. (92 post puffs)

**Row 3:** Ch 3, 2 dc in same st as beg ch-3, [sk post puff, 2 dc in next dc st] across to last 3 sts, sk next 2 sts, dc in last st, turn. (186 dc)

**Rows 4–9:** [Rep rows 2 and 3] 3 times. Fasten off at end of last row.

## Fringe

Matching colors to row ends, cut 2 10-inch strands for first and last row end. Cut 4 10-inch strands for all other row ends. (32 strands for each end of scarf)

On each short end of Scarf, place one **Lark's Head Knot** (see Special Stitches) on first and last row end; place 2 Lark's Head Knots on all other row ends.

Trim fringe as desired. ●

# Wasabi Popcorn Scarf for Her

## Skill Level
■■□□ EASY

## Finished Measurements
6½ inches wide x 44 inches long

## Gauge
16 sts = 4 inches; 7 rows = 4 inches

## Pattern Notes
Weave in loose ends as work progresses.

Chain-3 at beginning of row counts as first double crochet unless otherwise stated.

### Materials
- Premier Yarns Sweet Roll medium (worsted) weight acrylic yarn (5 oz/245 yds/140g per ball):
  1 ball #26 wasabi pop
- Size J/10/6mm crochet hook or size needed to obtain gauge
- Tapestry needle
- Measuring tape
- Scissors

**4 MEDIUM**

If there isn't enough yarn to repeat pattern rows 44 times, repeat pattern rows as many times as yarn will allow.

## Special Stitches

**Beginning popcorn (beg pc):** Ch 1, sc in first dc, 2 sc in next dc, drop lp from hook, insert hook in beg ch-1, draw dropped lp through.

**Popcorn (pc):** 2 sc in each of next 2 dc, drop lp from hook, insert hook in first sc made, draw dropped lp through.

## Scarf

**Row 1 (WS):** Leaving 24-inch strand at beg, ch 28, dc in **back bar** *(see illustration)* of 4th ch from hook *(3 sk chs count as a dc)*, [ch 2, sk next 2 chs, dc in back bar of each of next 2 chs] 6 times, turn. *(26 sts)*

**Back Bar of Chain**

**Row 2 (RS):** Beg pc *(see Special Stitches)*, [ch 3, sk next 2 chs, **pc** *(see Special Stitches)*] 6 times, turn. *(7 pc)*

**Row 3 (WS):** Ch 3 *(see Pattern Notes)*, dc in pc, [ch 2, sk next 2 chs, dc in next ch, dc in next pc] 6 times, turn. *(26 sts)*

**Rows 4–91:** [Rep rows 2 and 3] **44 times** *(see Pattern Notes)*. Fasten off at end of last row, leaving a 24-inch strand.

## Finishing

Fold rows 1–10 to back of work so foundation ch is touching row 20. Using long strand, sew beg ch to back of row 20.

Fold last row to back of work. Using long strand, sew in place. ●

# The Aah Back Scratcher

## Skill Level

 EASY

## Finished Measurements

4½ inches wide x 24 inches long, excluding handles

## Materials

- Premier Yarns Washi medium (worsted) weight polyester yarn (3½ oz/92 yds/100g per skein):
    - 1 skein #14 orange/white
- Aunt Lydia's Fashion size 3 crochet cotton (150 yds per ball):
    - 1 ball #201 white
- Sizes D/3/3.25mm and H/8/5mm crochet hooks or size needed to obtain gauge
- Tapestry needle
- Stitch marker
- Measuring tape
- Scissors

## Gauge

**With larger hook:** 5 (sc, ch 1) groups = 3 inches; 10 rows = 3 inches

## Pattern Notes

Weave in loose ends as work progresses.

Join with slip stitch as indicated unless otherwise stated.

## Scratcher

**Row 1 (WS):** With orange/white and larger hook, ch 81, sc in 2nd ch from hook, [sc in next ch, ch 1, sk next ch] 39 times, sc in last ch, turn. *(41 sc, 39 ch-1 sps)*

**Row 2:** Ch 1, sc in first st, [sc in next ch-1 sp, ch 1, sk next sc] 39 times, sc in last sc, turn.

**Rows 3–11:** [Rep row 2] 9 times.

**Row 12 (RS):** Ch 1, sc in first st, [sc in next ch-1 sp, ch 1, sk next sc] 39 times, sc in last sc, **change color** *(see Stitch Guide)* to white, turn to work across ends of rows. Fasten off orange/white.

## Edging

**Row 1 (RS):** With smaller hook, ch 1, sc in end of first row, [2 sc in end of next row, sc in end of next row] 5 times, 2 sc in end of last row, turn. *(18 sc)*

**Row 2:** Ch 1, sc in first st, place marker in last st made, sc in each st across, ch 40, turn, **join** *(see Pattern Notes)* in marked st. *(18 sc, 1 ch-40 sp)*

**Row 3:** Turn to work across unused lps of foundation ch, 2 sc in first unused lp, sc in each unused lp across to last unused lp, 2 sc in last unused lp, turn to work across ends of rows. *(82 sc)*

**Rows 4 & 5:** [Rep rows 1 and 2] once.

**Row 6:** Turn to work across row 12, 2 sc in first st, sc in each st across to last st, 2 sc in last st. *(82 sc)*

**Edging rnd:** Now working in rnd, *40 sc in ch-40 sp *(handle made)*, [(sc, ch 2, dc, tr) in next sc across row, sk next 2 sc] 27 times, sc in last sc of row, rep from * once, join in beg sc on handle. Fasten off. *(54 [sc, ch-2, dc, tr] groups, 2 handles)* ●

# Chains of Love Cowl

## Skill Level

 EASY

## Finished Measurements

7½ inches wide x 68 inches in circumference

## Materials

- Bernat Dazzle bulky (chunky) weight acrylic/polyester/wool yarn (3 oz/117 yds/85g per ball): 2 balls #7004 blue sky shine

  **5 BULKY**

- Size P/Q/15mm crochet hook or size needed to obtain gauge
- Tapestry needle
- Stitch marker
- Measuring tape
- Scissors

## Gauge

7 sts = 4 inches; 7 rows = 4 inches

## Pattern Notes

Weave in loose ends as work progresses.

Mark first stitch of round, move marker up with each round.

Work in continuous rounds, do not turn or join unless otherwise stated.

## Special Stitch

**Split single crochet (split sc):** Insert hook between legs of st, yo, draw through st, yo, draw through both lps on hook.

## Cowl

**Rnd 1 (RS):** Leaving 10-inch strand at beg for sewing, ch 121, sc in **back bar** (see illustration) of 2nd ch from hook, **place marker in sc just made** (see Pattern Notes), sc in back bar of each rem ch across, being careful not to twist sts, **split sc** (see Special Stitch) in first st to form ring. (120 sc)

**Back Bar of Chain**

**Rnd 2:** [Ch 2, sk next 2 sts, split sc in next st] 40 times, **do not join** (see Pattern Notes).

**Rnd 3:** [Ch 2, sk next 2 chs, split sc in next st] 40 times.

**Rnds 4–13:** [Rep rnd 3] 10 times.

**Rnd 14:** Sc in back bar of each of first 2 chs, [split sc in next st, sc in back bar of each of next 2 chs] 39 times, sl st between legs of last st to join. Fasten off.

With beg strand, sew bottom of rnd 1 tog. ●

# Braided Wonders Headband

## Skill Level

 EASY

## Finished Measurements

2½ inches wide x 20½ inches long

## Materials

- Patons Alpaca Blend bulky (chunky) weight yarn (3½oz/ 155 yds/100g per skein): 1 skein #01010 iceberg
- Size I/9/5.5mm crochet hook or size needed to obtain gauge
- Tapestry needle
- Measuring tape
- Scissors

**5 BULKY**

## Gauge
16 sts = 4 inches; 7 rows = 2½ inches

## Pattern Note
Weave in loose ends as work progresses.

## Headband
**Row 1 (RS):** Ch 81, sc in **back bar** (see illustration) of 2nd ch from hook and in back bar of each rem ch across, turn. (80 sts)

**Back Bar of Chain**

**Row 2:** Ch 1, [**bpsc** (see Stitch Guide) around post of next st, **fpsc** (see Stitch Guide) around post of next st] 11 times, bpsc around post of next st, sc in each of next 32 sts, [bpsc around post of next st, fpsc around post of next st] 11 times, bpsc around post of next st, sc in last st, turn.

**Row 3:** Ch 1, sc in first st, [fpsc around post of next post st, bpsc around post of next post st] 11 times, fpsc around post of next post st, sc in each of next 32 sts, [fpsc around post of next post st, bpsc around post of next post st] 11 times, fpsc around post of next post st, sc in last st, turn.

**Row 4:** Ch 1, sc in first st, [bpsc around post of next post st, fpsc around post of next post st] 11 times, bpsc around post of next post st, sl st in next st, ch 30, sk next 30 sts, sl st in next st, leaving rem 24 sts unworked, turn. (56 sts)

**Row 5:** Ch 1, sk sl st, [sc in back bar of next ch] 30 times, sl st in next sl st, leaving rem 24 sts unworked, turn. (31 sts)

**Row 6:** Ch 1, sk sl st, sc in each of next 30 sts, sl st in ch-1 st, turn.

**Row 7:** Rep row 6.

**Row 8:** Ch 1, sc in sl st, ch 30, sk next 30 sts, sc in next ch-1 st, working around post of post sts on row 3, [bpsc around post of next post st, fpsc around post of next post st] 11 times, bpsc around post of next post st, sc in last st, turn. (56 sts)

**Row 9:** Ch 1, sc in first st, [fpsc around post of next post st, bpsc around post of next post st] 11 times, fpsc around post of next post st, sc in next sc, [sc in back bar of next ch] 30 times, sc in next sc, working around post of post sts on row 4, [fpsc around post of next post st, bpsc around post of next post st] 11 times, fpsc around post of next post st, sc in last st, turn. (80 sts)

**Rows 10 & 11:** [Rep rows 2 and 3] once. Fasten off at end of last row, leaving long strand for sewing.

## Braiding
Turn fabric so straps are vertical.

**1.** Fold bottom, where straps are joined, up and through sp between center strap and right strap.

**2.** Fold left strap over center strap.

**3.** Fold right strap over center strap.

**4.** Rep step 2.

**5.** Fold bottom, where straps are joined, up and through sp between left strap and center strap. (After step 5, straps below braiding area will be untwisted.)

**6.** Rep step 3.

**7.** Rep step 2.

**8.** Rep step 3.

Rep steps 1–5.

## Finishing
Fold Headband in half with RS facing. With long strand, sew row ends tog. ●

# STITCH GUIDE

*Need help?* ▶ StitchGuide.com • ILLUSTRATED GUIDES • HOW-TO VIDEOS

## STITCH ABBREVIATIONS

beg . . . . . . . . . . . . . . . . . . . . . . . . . . . . begin/begins/beginning
bpdc . . . . . . . . . . . . . . . . . . . . . . . . back post double crochet
bpsc . . . . . . . . . . . . . . . . . . . . . . . . .back post single crochet
bptr . . . . . . . . . . . . . . . . . . . . . . . . .back post treble crochet
CC. . . . . . . . . . . . . . . . . . . . . . . . . . . . . . . . . contrasting color
ch(s) . . . . . . . . . . . . . . . . . . . . . . . . . . . . . . . . . . . . .chain(s)
ch- . . . . . . . . . . . . . . . . . . . . . . . . . .refers to chain or space
         previously made (i.e., ch-1 space)
ch sp(s) . . . . . . . . . . . . . . . . . . . . . . . . . . . . . chain space(s)
cl(s) . . . . . . . . . . . . . . . . . . . . . . . . . . . . . . . . . . . cluster(s)
cm . . . . . . . . . . . . . . . . . . . . . . . . . . . . . . . . . . . centimeter(s)
dc . . . . . . . . . . . . . . . . . . . . . . . . double crochet (singular/plural)
dc dec. . . . . . . . . . . . . . . . . . . . . . . double crochet 2 or more
         stitches together, as indicated
dec. . . . . . . . . . . . . . . . . . . . . . decrease/decreases/decreasing
dtr . . . . . . . . . . . . . . . . . . . . . . . . . . . . double treble crochet
ext . . . . . . . . . . . . . . . . . . . . . . . . . . . . . . . . . . . . . .extended
fpdc . . . . . . . . . . . . . . . . . . . . . . . front post double crochet
fpsc . . . . . . . . . . . . . . . . . . . . . . . . front post single crochet
fptr . . . . . . . . . . . . . . . . . . . . . . . . front post treble crochet
g . . . . . . . . . . . . . . . . . . . . . . . . . . . . . . . . . . . . . . . .gram(s)
hdc . . . . . . . . . . . . . . . . . . . . . . . . . . . . . half double crochet
hdc dec . . . . . . . . . . . . . . half double crochet 2 or more
         stitches together, as indicated
inc . . . . . . . . . . . . . . . . . . . . . . increase/increases/increasing
lp(s) . . . . . . . . . . . . . . . . . . . . . . . . . . . . . . . . . . . . .loop(s)
MC . . . . . . . . . . . . . . . . . . . . . . . . . . . . . . . . . . . .main color
mm . . . . . . . . . . . . . . . . . . . . . . . . . . . . . . . . . . .millimeter(s)
oz . . . . . . . . . . . . . . . . . . . . . . . . . . . . . . . . . . . . . .ounce(s)
pc . . . . . . . . . . . . . . . . . . . . . . . . . . . . . . . . . . . . . popcorn(s)
rem . . . . . . . . . . . . . . . . . . . . . remain/remains/remaining
rep(s) . . . . . . . . . . . . . . . . . . . . . . . . . . . . . . . . . . .repeat(s)
rnd(s) . . . . . . . . . . . . . . . . . . . . . . . . . . . . . . . . . . . round(s)
RS . . . . . . . . . . . . . . . . . . . . . . . . . . . . . . . . . . . . . .right side
sc . . . . . . . . . . . . . . . . . . single crochet (singular/plural)
sc dec. . . . . . . . . . . . . . . . . . .single crochet 2 or more
         stitches together, as indicated
sk . . . . . . . . . . . . . . . . . . . . . . . . . . . . .skip/skipped/skipping
sl st(s) . . . . . . . . . . . . . . . . . . . . . . . . . . . . . . slip stitch(es)
sp(s) . . . . . . . . . . . . . . . . . . . . . . . . . . . . . . space(s)/spaced
st(s) . . . . . . . . . . . . . . . . . . . . . . . . . . . . . . . . . . stitch(es)
tog . . . . . . . . . . . . . . . . . . . . . . . . . . . . . . . . . . . . .together
tr. . . . . . . . . . . . . . . . . . . . . . . . . . . . . . . . . . treble crochet
trtr. . . . . . . . . . . . . . . . . . . . . . . . . . . . . . . . . .triple treble
WS . . . . . . . . . . . . . . . . . . . . . . . . . . . . . . . . . . . wrong side
yd(s) . . . . . . . . . . . . . . . . . . . . . . . . . . . . . . . . . . . . .yard(s)
yo . . . . . . . . . . . . . . . . . . . . . . . . . . . . . . . . . . . . . .yarn over

## YARN CONVERSION

| OUNCES TO GRAMS | | GRAMS TO OUNCES | |
|---|---|---|---|
| 1 | 28.4 | 25 | ⅞ |
| 2 | 56.7 | 40 | 1⅔ |
| 3 | 85.0 | 50 | 1¾ |
| 4 | 113.4 | 100 | 3½ |

| UNITED STATES | | UNITED KINGDOM |
|---|---|---|
| sl st (slip stitch) | = | sc (single crochet) |
| sc (single crochet) | = | dc (double crochet) |
| hdc (half double crochet) | = | htr (half treble crochet) |
| dc (double crochet) | = | tr (treble crochet) |
| tr (treble crochet) | = | dtr (double treble crochet) |
| dtr (double treble crochet) | = | ttr (triple treble crochet) |
| skip | = | miss |

**Reverse single crochet (reverse sc):** Ch 1, sk first st, working from left to right, insert hook in next st from front to back, draw up lp on hook, yo and draw through both lps on hook.

**Chain (ch):** Yo, pull through lp on hook.

**Single crochet (sc):** Insert hook in st, yo, pull through st, yo, pull through both lps on hook.

**Double crochet (dc):** Yo, insert hook in st, yo, pull through st, [yo, pull through 2 lps] twice.

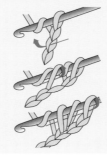

**Front loop (front lp) Back loop (back lp)**

Front Loop    Back Loop

**Front post stitch (fp): Back post stitch (bp):** When working post st, insert hook from right to left around post of st on previous row.

Back    Front

Post of Stitch

**Half double crochet (hdc):** Yo, insert hook in st, yo, pull through st, yo, pull through all 3 lps on hook.

**Double treble crochet (dtr):** Yo 3 times, insert hook in st, yo, pull through st, [yo, pull through 2 lps] 4 times.

**Slip stitch (sl st):** Insert hook in st, pull through both lps on hook.

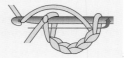

**Chain color change (ch color change)** Yo with new color, draw through last lp on hook.

**Double crochet color change (dc color change)** Drop first color, yo with new color, draw through last 2 lps of st.

**Treble crochet (tr):** Yo twice, insert hook in st, yo, pull through st, [yo, pull through 2 lps] 3 times.

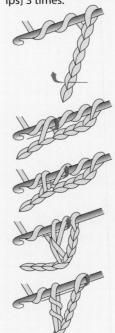

**Single crochet decrease (sc dec):** (Insert hook, yo, draw lp through) in each of the sts indicated, yo, draw through all lps on hook.

Example of 2-sc dec

**Half double crochet decrease (hdc dec):** (Yo, insert hook, yo, draw lp through) in each of the sts indicated, yo, draw through all lps on hook.

Example of 2-hdc dec

**Double crochet decrease (dc dec):** (Yo, insert hook, yo, draw lp through, yo, draw through 2 lps on hook) in each of the sts indicated, yo, draw through all lps on hook.

Example of 2-dc dec

**Treble crochet decrease (tr dec):** Holding back last lp of each st, tr in each of the sts indicated, yo, pull through all lps on hook.

Example of 2-tr dec

# Metric Conversion Charts

## METRIC CONVERSIONS

| | | | | |
|---|---|---|---|---|
| yards | x | .9144 | = | metres (m) |
| yards | x | 91.44 | = | centimetres (cm) |
| inches | x | 2.54 | = | centimetres (cm) |
| inches | x | 25.40 | = | millimetres (mm) |
| inches | x | .0254 | = | metres (m) |

| | | | | |
|---|---|---|---|---|
| centimetres | x | .3937 | = | inches |
| metres | x | 1.0936 | = | yards |

## INCHES INTO MILLIMETRES & CENTIMETRES (Rounded off slightly)

| inches | mm | cm | inches | cm | inches | cm | inches | cm |
|---|---|---|---|---|---|---|---|---|
| 1/8 | 3 | 0.3 | 5 | 12.5 | 21 | 53.5 | 38 | 96.5 |
| 1/4 | 6 | 0.6 | 5 1/2 | 14 | 22 | 56 | 39 | 99 |
| 3/8 | 10 | 1 | 6 | 15 | 23 | 58.5 | 40 | 101.5 |
| 1/2 | 13 | 1.3 | 7 | 18 | 24 | 61 | 41 | 104 |
| 5/8 | 15 | 1.5 | 8 | 20.5 | 25 | 63.5 | 42 | 106.5 |
| 3/4 | 20 | 2 | 9 | 23 | 26 | 66 | 43 | 109 |
| 7/8 | 22 | 2.2 | 10 | 25.5 | 27 | 68.5 | 44 | 112 |
| 1 | 25 | 2.5 | 11 | 28 | 28 | 71 | 45 | 114.5 |
| 1 1/4 | 32 | 3.2 | 12 | 30.5 | 29 | 73.5 | 46 | 117 |
| 1 1/2 | 38 | 3.8 | 13 | 33 | 30 | 76 | 47 | 119.5 |
| 1 3/4 | 45 | 4.5 | 14 | 35.5 | 31 | 79 | 48 | 122 |
| 2 | 50 | 5 | 15 | 38 | 32 | 81.5 | 49 | 124.5 |
| 2 1/2 | 65 | 6.5 | 16 | 40.5 | 33 | 84 | 50 | 127 |
| 3 | 75 | 7.5 | 17 | 43 | 34 | 86.5 | | |
| 3 1/2 | 90 | 9 | 18 | 46 | 35 | 89 | | |
| 4 | 100 | 10 | 19 | 48.5 | 36 | 91.5 | | |
| 4 1/2 | 115 | 11.5 | 20 | 51 | 37 | 94 | | |

## KNITTING NEEDLES CONVERSION CHART

| Canada/U.S. | 0 | 1 | 2 | 3 | 4 | 5 | 6 | 7 | 8 | 9 | 10 | 10½ | 11 | 13 | 15 |
|---|---|---|---|---|---|---|---|---|---|---|---|---|---|---|---|
| Metric (mm) | 2 | 2¼ | 2¾ | 3¼ | 3½ | 3¾ | 4 | 4½ | 5 | 5½ | 6 | 6½ | 8 | 9 | 10 |

## CROCHET HOOKS CONVERSION CHART

| Canada/U.S. | 1/B | 2/C | 3/D | 4/E | 5/F | 6/G | 8/H | 9/I | 10/J | 10½/K | N |
|---|---|---|---|---|---|---|---|---|---|---|---|
| Metric (mm) | 2.25 | 2.75 | 3.25 | 3.5 | 3.75 | 4.25 | 5 | 5.5 | 6 | 6.5 | 9.0 |

Annie's® *30 Gifts in 30 Days* is published by Annie's, 306 East Parr Road, Berne, IN 46711. Printed in USA. Copyright © 2017 Annie's. All rights reserved. This publication may not be reproduced in part or in whole without written permission from the publisher.

**RETAIL STORES:** If you would like to carry this publication or any other Annie's publication, visit AnniesWSL.com.

Every effort has been made to ensure that the instructions in this publication are complete and accurate. We cannot, however, take responsibility for human error, typographical mistakes or variations in individual work. Please visit AnniesCustomerService.com to check for pattern updates.

ISBN: 978-1-59012-850-3

2 3 4 5 6 7 8 9